It's
GRAMPA'S TIME

A Blueprint for the Family Patriarch
— Changing the World
Through the Next Generation

Ahelia Publishing
Helena, Montana

AHELIA
PUBLISHING, LLC

It's GRAMPA'S TIME

A Blueprint for the Family Patriarch
— Changing the World
Through the Next Generation

CALVIN C. ELLERBY

It's Grampa's Time—A Blueprint for the Family Patriarch to Change the World Through the Next Generation

Copyright © 2018 Calvin C. Ellerby

ISBN# 978-1-988001-34-0

1. God 2. Christianity 3. Religion 4. Family 5. Patriarch

Printed in the United States of America
Published in the United States of America

www.aheliapublishing.com
aheliapublishing@outlook.com

AHELIA
PUBLISHING, LLC

To receive your **FREE** *Grampa's Time* Self-study booklet, just email cal@grampastime.com and request a copy. I will gladly send you one if it will assist you in your journey of becoming the patriarch God has called you to be.

For speaking engagements, workshop presentations, or conferences, please contact Cal at calellerby@nucleus.com.

Watch for the upcoming small group study resource and other books designed to encourage and enhance your walk with Christ as the head of your home, your church, and your community.

The "Grampa's Time" ministry exists to:

"Enlist, Equip, Encourage, and Empower 1,000,000 Grandfathers and Fathers to Lay hands on their Grandchildren and Children, Speaking the Blessing of God into their Lives."

Table of Contents

SECTION 1   THE FOUNDATION

SECTION 2   THE IMPARTATION

SECTION 3   THE COMMISSION

Foreword

ON A BEAUTIFUL EVENING IN JULY 1980, I HAD A FRONT ROW SEAT TO WATCH as God powerfully orchestrated the transformation of a young man's life. That night, Cal Ellerby responded to an invitation to surrender his life to Christ. This was no ordinary life either, nor was a deep, purposeful relationship between myself and this man even remotely probable. At that moment, God was faithfully honoring the consistent prayers of Wilbur Ellerby, the author's own grampa, demonstrating proof-positive the very essence of Cal's message. Some thirty-eight years later, I've finished reading through the manuscript you now hold in your hands as a book—incidentally, a message that has the potential to radically impact your life and change the course of history.

Throughout the years, I've observed Cal faithfully respond to God's call on his life, complete with seasons of wrestling under what has become evident as a significant mantle. I have been fortunate to journey alongside Cal, listening as he has processed visions of healthy, effective, vibrant churches, church leadership, and men in general, always with a mix of passion, conviction, and humility, yet a forced discipline demonstrating a level of patient nurture that is not particularly a natural or preferred one.

Whispers from God often fall on deaf ears. People are busy and distracted by the very lives, responsibilities, and tasks we find before us. Fortunately, there are leaders such as Cal, who are driven to hear these whispers from God and avail themselves as a conduit through which God can flow His love and purposes. "It's Grampa's Time" is the manifestation of one of those whispers.

This specific whisper is both profound and timely. As you read, you will find yourself drawn into a story masterfully woven together with a focus on biblical history, order, structure, and consistency. The challenge you will find yourself forced to embrace or reject will itself eventually become a fact of history. While you get to choose your response, you will not defy the inevitable outcome of that chosen response. Leadership is not for the casually interested. It will always extract more than we intend to invest. Our role as leaders was not our decision. Being a patriarch is not a chosen position, but rather one determined by God Himself. "… male and female he created them" (Genesis 1:27). In current society, the male and female thing is a major issue. Cal effectively unpacks God's order and rightly identifies patriarchs, along with the crucial role we have been assigned from the beginning of time. Cal courageously does so in spite of, and in direct contradiction to what society is desperately insisting upon as today's new reality.

Max De Pree[1] in his website of building foundations said, "The number one responsibility of a leader is to define reality." Each chapter are you are about to read is rich with foundational understanding, practical insight, demonstrated application, and relevance for this very moment. 1 Chronicles 12:32 states, "… from Issachar, men who understood the times and knew what Israel should do …" David was fortunate to have men around him who understood the times and knew what to do! Who among us today understands our current times and knows what to do? I believe this book's author may well be such a person.

It's not uncommon to hear people state the obvious, whether good or bad, but it is less common to hear people also state what we should do in light of the obvious. For most of us, we are painfully aware the family unit has come under attack; this is not a recent phenomenon. Cal rightly acknowledges that for quite some time, we have watched our societal leaders and government undermine and, in essence, destroy the fiber and foundation of the family. Men, in particular, have been marginalized and even neutralized in modern society. Rooted in a sense of fear, men have abdicated their God-given roles and responsibilities to other sources and influences. Cal compellingly admonishes men to rise up against this illusion (lie) created by our archenemy, and resume our God-ordained role as patriarchs.

All men, grampas in particular, need encouragement and support in re-establishing their place and purpose on the earth. As you read, you will find testimony declaring a new-found sense of hope and purpose among men who have heard and responded to the message contained in these pages. Not only does your life matter, you are an essential component of God's master plan for creation. Cal provides a powerful explanation of man's DNA being biologically linked to God; no other aspect of God's creation can boast this reality.

---

[1] De Pree, Max. (2004). *Leadership is an Art.* New York, NY: Currency.

As we observe the ongoing slaughter of biblical values and principles occurring daily on the earth, it can feel somewhat hopeless. In reality, the task and challenge before us of turning this nation back to the values and principles it was founded upon is daunting. *It's Grampa's Time* will breathe new hope and energy into your soul as you discover the pattern God has established in generating His blessing and provision throughout time. In a day and age where confusion and absurdity are normalized, Cal brilliantly reminds us that God is not a God of disorder or confusion. Take courage and prepare to experience renewal and passion in partnering with God for His rich, abundant blessing on our kids, grandkids, and future generations.

To "bless" is to invite God's presence in increasing measure and abundance (Chapter 4). Might you be one of the one million men Cal is trusting God to raise up for the express purpose of invoking the powerful blessing of God? I implore you to carefully consider joining this mandate. As you read, you will be equipped with a systematic process for invoking God's blessing upon your own grandkids, but even beyond your own, to the multitude of kids who have no functional dad or grampa. Imagine the impact as we collectively lock arms and strategically invite God's blessing in increasing measure and abundance. This is more than just a nice idea; it is crucial for our kids. Friend, Grampa, you are an essential part of ensuring God's presence and purposes for current and future generations. It's not just any old time in history; *It's Grampa's Time!*

Wayne Durksen
Kids Matter Leadership, CEO

Thanks To ...

I want to acknowledge the support and help that I have received from special people who have cheered this project on in very meaningful ways.

My brother Dallas has been a patriarch in my life for many, many years. His encouragement, support, and incredible generosity have not only kept me motivated, but have made the book a possibility in very tangible ways. The faithfulness to his gifts and God's call on his life have been instrumental in making sure this project came to completion.

To my sister Bernice, who has read and reread the manuscript, offering insightful opinions and helps in the writing of the book.

To my brother Marlon and sister Brenda, who are living proof of the importance of a godly heritage.

To my mother, Elaine, who has always believed I could accomplish anything.

To my dad, Albert, who went to Heaven in 1999 but was a real-life example of what it means to be a man.

To Tim and Melody Ellerby, who have so generously supported this ministry.

To the many supporters of the *Grampa's Time* vision, who have shared their life stories and contributed financially to the ministry since its inception.

Dedication

It's Grampa's Time is dedicated to my amazing wife Mary, who has for over thirty-five years, continually encouraged me and supported the many ideas and promptings I have had, with nothing but love and optimism.

To my three wonderful children, Denton (Sherisse), Keaton (Lauren), and Tiffany (Pat), who have taught me and continue to teach me about life, love, and family.

Oh, then there are these guys: Nixon, Callaghan, Kensington, and Beckett. They are the people for whom this book exists—my fabulous grandchildren, whose future I take very seriously. They are tomorrow's men and women of God.

Section One

THE FOUNDATION

IT'S GRAMPA'S TIME

Chapter 1

The word of the LORD came to me, saying, "Before I formed you in the womb I knew you, before you were born I set you apart; I appointed you as a prophet to the nations."

Jeremiah 1:4-5

GRAMPA'S BIBLE. IT IS WITHOUT QUESTION ONE OF THE MOST TREASURED possessions I own. I keep it in a blue plastic bag on my office bookshelf to protect it from the elements, because it is like an ancient manuscript. The note on the inside cover says, "J.W. Ellerby, Christmas 1946."

The cover of this beautiful, old book is made of some sort of simulated leather, which has deteriorated over the years and is literally falling apart. The pages are yellow and often detached from the binding; many are torn and tattered. As with any special possession, repairs have been attempted by reattaching the torn pages with tape that is now clouded over, making the print beneath it impossible to read. I can just feel Grampa's emotion as he sought to restore and prevent further deterioration of this sacred document. It was his connection to God. It was a part of him.

The constant handling has left those pages frayed and fragile, and throughout the entire Bible, there are handwritten notes on papers inserted into specially selected locations, with comments and observations about the Scriptures on those pages.

The Gospels of Luke and John, the book of Acts, Romans, 1st and 2nd Corinthians, Ephesians, and especially the Book of Revelation, have pages nearly worn through, and have countless references and observations written on the margins of each page. There are notes in red ink, blue ink, and in pencil. There are words underlined and circled. Some are underlined twice, with arrows pointing to other correlating Scriptures that have been written in for further study and confirmation.

It's fascinating to me to identify the themes of Grampa's passions and interests in the Scriptures. It's obvious from reading through his notes and observing what he read most and what he highlighted, that there were spiritual truths that had profoundly impacted his life and journey with Jesus.

Both Grampa and my grandmother had a powerful encounter with God. When I look at his notes and the portions of Scripture he read most often, it is obvious that he was enthralled with the power of the Holy Spirit. I know from speaking to my siblings and to my aunts and uncles, that Grampa also loved the message of the Name of Jesus, the grace of God, divine healing, and the return of Christ at the Second Coming. His Bible was a photograph of his heart. It is unquestionably a reflection of his character and his longing to know God and His love for the world. Grampa's Bible literally tells his life story.

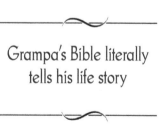

Grampa's Bible literally tells his life story

I was only seven years old when grampa Ellerby passed away. He was seventy-three and was known to be a man who loved to laugh and tell stories. He wasn't tall, but rather thick and strong, with large hands and a balding head; at least that's how I remember him.

Grampa homesteaded on the bald, cold prairies of central Alberta in 1911 and lived in a one-room sod shack with his two brothers, for thirteen years. He was a farmer who married late and raised a family of seven children. He continued to farm until his passing, but on January 1st, 1939, he became a licensed minister. He proceeded to travel into the northern native communities of Alberta to supply clothing and food, to preach the gospel, and to pray for the sick in those communities. He was a man ahead of his time. He printed a monthly newsletter he sent up to the communities he served and to the many people who followed his ministry. I vividly remember the old typewriter and the printing Gestetner he used to produce his newsletter. When I think of it now, I marvel at his vision and passion for the work of God and his deep love of the First Nations people.

There were many experiences in my grandfather's life which made that old Bible so valuable. Many were joyous and exhilarating, but there were plenty of trying times as well. I believe it was in 1956 that my grandmother became very ill, and as I understand the story, Grampa Ellerby literally carried Grandma out of the hospital and drove two hundred miles to a crusade where he prayed for her condition. She was completely healed of what her doctor had told her was likely a cancerous tumor in her pancreas. Grandma Ellerby died in 1985 of old age.

Looking at his Bible and reading through it takes me to a place in my imagination that unveils something very precious to me. His Bible tells its own story. It gives me insight into a man who loved God with all of his heart in a deep, personal, and experiential way—a man who knew first-hand, his living Savior. It gives me insight into his heart, into his life, and maybe more importantly, into my own life.

I imagine my grampa, sitting at night after a long, hard day's work on the farm, with a coal oil lamp, resting in his chair with his Bible held close to his face. I imagine him reading, praying, and worshipping Jesus with tears streaming down his cheeks, with internal groans of gratitude and love for a God whom he knew was real and who loved him unconditionally. I imagine

Grampa Ellerby praying for his children and his grandchildren that they too, would know Jesus the way he did. I imagine him believing God for men and women of God in his own family tree that would be servants in the Kingdom. I envision him praying that his family, and their families, would commit their lives to the service of Christ in order that the world, for generations to come, would be changed and impacted by the grace, mercy, and forgiveness found in the wonderful and glorious name of Jesus.

When I think of my grandfather, I can't help but think of King David when he cried out to God in Psalm 71:18:

Even when I am old and gray, do not forsake me, my God, till I declare your power to the next generation, your mighty acts to all who are yet to come.

Just as David did, I believe my grandfather had vision for the next generation. He was a leader who recognized his personal responsibility to the next generation, and yet he recognized his utter dependency on God to impact that next generation. In some intrinsic way, he longed to leave a legacy to the generations who were going to follow him; that his influence and his relationship with Jesus might be carried on in their lives.

Jonathon Wilbur Ellerby was a true spiritual patriarch.

My Journey

On November 24th, 1985, I was ordained as a minister in the small community of Melfort, Saskatchewan. My grandfather would have been very proud, I'm sure. I was one more family member who had been motivated by the Lord to serve Him in full-time ministry. My grandfather had been gone for nearly twenty years. I had never spoken to him about ministry, or even what it meant to be a Christian. He never left me notes or instructions or ideas or connections. I was just one of several grandchildren. I'm positive he loved each of us equally (well, maybe my sister Bernice a little more), but there is no recollection of any direct influence he had on my life.

Even though I have no memorable experience with Grampa Ellerby's instruction or tutelage, it is interesting to me how spiritual affections carry on from generation to generation. There were not only a few conversions, but there have been many, many cousins and siblings who have had a passionate desire to serve the Lord in His Kingdom. Many of my relatives currently, or at one point in their lives, have served in full-time ministry. My wife Mary and I ended up pastoring for nearly twenty years. Go figure.

Here's where my story starts to take on its own life and begins to lay the foundation for this book.

After pastoring for all those years and being in the business community for about fifteen years after that, I came to a point in my life where I found myself once again striving to know the mind and heart of God in a fresh way. He was leading me down a new path of discovery. Longing to understand His ways in our current generation set me on somewhat of a quest.

My pursuits led me to ask the Lord this question:

"What does success look like?"

I have since changed the word *success* to the word *fruitfulness,* because that is what I was really longing to discern. If that sounds like a deep subject, please don't misunderstand me. That really wasn't my intent. It was more of an observation question at that point in my life. My kids were grown, my life was stable and fulfilled, and I was a first-time grandfather myself. There were no issues to contend with, just a longing to know the ways of God more intimately and deeply.

Every day for a number of months, I would walk and ask the Lord to give me a greater understanding of what it meant to be fruitful in life. It was a wonderful time of sensing the leadership of the Holy Spirit, resulting in many insights and realizations of simple truths in more profound ways. There really is nothing like the whisper of the Spirit of God into your heart and thoughts when you are quiet and open to Him. I felt like I was on an adventure. It was really a very cool experience. The principles that became clear to me are the framework of a future book. I should divulge some of those principles here, but they are for another time—and a completely different subject.

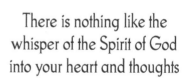

There is nothing like the whisper of the Spirit of God into your heart and thoughts

The relevance of that journey, however, is this. It began to open my heart to hear the voice of God in a way that I had not heard for many years. I am convinced that the sovereign leadership of Christ was preparing me to hear something unexpected; a totally new plan that could change the world as we know it. I had to be retooled to be able to hear what God wanted to do with the vision He was about to give me.

When I left pastoring in the year 2000, I was pretty much burned out and had decided I was done with working with people. In fact, I literally said to the Lord, "I am done working with people." I wasn't sure how to make it more clear than that. I was tired and empty. I felt that I had nothing left to give. I concluded that going into business would be more rewarding, lucrative, and satisfying. I didn't need people or the ministry.

Eventually, however, after all those years away from full-time ministry, for some reason I felt compelled to ask the Lord another question.

"What does fruitfulness look like?"

If you have ever been on such a journey, you probably know it always ends up with God challenging you with something you assumed was dead and buried. I was no exception. I was about to find out that when you ask God questions, He sometimes answers in life-altering ways.

ENCOUNTER ONE:
The Midnight Whisper

It began one night in the middle of a deep sleep. I woke up and heard a very distinct voice. It wasn't audible, but it might as well have been. The words I heard were as though they were the conclusion of a conversation I had with God nearly fifteen years earlier.

"You might not need people, but people need you!"

Now, in my humble opinion, that's a horrible thing to say to a guy like me in the middle of the night. I had spent the last several years avoiding the idea of being involved with Kingdom service and had no intention of starting again now. I concluded that whatever I ate the night before had obviously caused me to have a dream, or worse, a nightmare.

A few days after I heard that "voice," I was telling my brother about what I had heard. Normally he is my comic relief in life, but on this occasion, he looked at me in a very serious way and replied with, "You had better be careful, that might have been God." He was right. As much as I wasn't crazy about where this was going, I would be a complete fool to assume that if God had begun something, He wouldn't take it further.

Somewhat reluctantly, I went to the Lord with a conditional acknowledgment of what I had come to assume was His voice. When you have worked hard at shaping your world, it can be very uncomfortable when God starts to rearrange it. I don't like uncomfortable. I did, however, have a desire to discover the mind of God, and it seemed clear that this experience was very much a part of that discovery. I was now relatively open to hearing the next part of what I felt was the opening volley of the Lord.

This is what I prayed:

"Lord, I want to do something significant in the Kingdom that is consistent with my gifts, and that I would enjoy doing."

When I read that now, I realize what an arrogant statement that is. It's kind of like, "OK God, listen up, here's my plan." Thank you, Lord, for Your mercy and Your patience! If the truth was known, what I really was saying was, "God, I am interested in serving You, but I am not going pastoring again. I'm just saying."

That was a defining moment for me. It was the first time in many years that I was at all open to what God might have me do for the Kingdom. It was exciting and yet curious at the same time.

ENCOUNTER TWO:
It's Grampa's Time

In October of 2013, my wife and I were holidaying with some friends in Mexico. We were about halfway through our time there when again, I had a middle-of-the-night encounter with what I have concluded was a second specific word from the Lord. This time the prompting was short, yet incredibly clear. The word was,

I recall being wide awake and thinking to myself, *This is a game changer.* I knew exactly what the Lord meant. I obviously did not have all the pieces, but I knew instinctively what God was saying. I knew and believed that if I would be faithful to this call, I could be a part of a movement that could literally change the course of our entire society. God had a plan and He was inviting me to be a part of it. Can there be anything more exciting?

Over the next few weeks, I began to discern more and more of what God meant by the statement "It's Grampa's Time." The Lord helped me to see that the patriarchal role of grandfathers has been largely displaced in our society and how contrary that is to God's ultimate design of the way the family is intended to grow. It was suddenly obvious to me that the spiritual forces who oppose our faith in Christ had, in fact, been systematically dismantling the role of the patriarch in the family.

My immediate question was, "Why?" It was at that point I realized the patriarch literally holds within his hands an instrumental and strategic part in executing God's blessing for all generations. It is Grampa's responsibility to be a conduit of God's blessing to all generations that will follow him. This was the secret to my own call to the ministry. This was Grampa Ellerby's legacy. His heritage. His role in God's bigger plan.

The transition and transfer of God's power from one generation to the next

The spiritual forces of darkness understand better than we do that if they can eliminate the influence of the patriarch, they can minimize the impact of God's favor on the youngest of the generations. The elimination of the patriarch's influence makes the following generations vulnerable to the assaults and attacks of our spiritual enemy.

As I prayed about this revelation and sought to understand more fully what God was saying, I began to see a blueprint take shape. It was making perfect sense. We were losing a battle because the enemy was slowly but surely dismantling God's divine order in the family. It is like the old adage of boiling a frog by slowly turning up the heat. I was beginning to see the stove had to be turned off. It is time to restore our alignment with God's plan.

Jacob, Joseph, and His Boys

As I will share in later chapters, I felt that God was directing me to the story of Jacob and his son Joseph in Genesis 48. In that chapter, the plan for passing God's blessing on to the next generation is clearly laid out. I have since defined it as the **5 Step Blueprint to Change the World.** It is simple, yet profound. It is practical, yet mystical. Jacob demonstrated this blueprint in one of the most touching stories of the Old Testament.

After hearing of Jacob's imminent passing, Joseph immediately called his two sons, Ephraim and Manasseh, to his side to make their way to his father, who was now on his deathbed. His reasons were deeper than just to pay his respects and say goodbye. Joseph understood something much more sacred had to take place before his father went to Heaven. Joseph understood that his dad had something that only he could give to his children. Joseph's request was simple. Paraphrased, he said, "Dad, don't die until you have laid your hands on my two boys and spoken the blessing of God into their lives."

Wow, that is a powerful picture. This is the transition and transfer of God's power from one generation to the next. That's it. That is God's plan for today; the mobilization of men of God passing His blessing on to the next generation, in order that they might be used by God to establish His Kingdom authority and presence throughout the earth. I'm not sure about you, but I'm in.

The Blueprint

The Scriptures lay out a magnificent blueprint for this transference of God's blessing. Furthermore, it is shown multiple times throughout the Bible as a model of the way God intends for the family structure to be used as an instrument for developing His Lordship in every period of time. Unfortunately, our society has, for the most part, missed it. We have been victims of a diabolical ploy to displace the heads of the family tree—the patriarchs. So, what does the blueprint look like?

5 Step Blueprint

Step 1: Jacob understood his <u>patriarchal role</u>

Step 2: He understood what the <u>Blessing of God</u> meant

Step 3: He understood the power of <u>laying on of hands</u>

Step 4: He understood the power of the <u>spoken word</u>

Step 5: He imparted the <u>Blessing</u> in faith

As this blueprint became more and more clear to me, I realized that God's desire and call was to mobilize men across North America to make a commitment to exactly replicate the pattern of Jacob. I am convinced that if we can help men see themselves in the role God has appointed them, and give them tools to assist them in their responsibility, we can see a society-altering shift that will unleash a move of God that has never been seen before in our nations.

ENCOUNTER THREE:
Mobilize 1,000,000 Grandfathers

During the third middle-of-the-night encounter, I felt the Lord said:

"Mobilize 1,000,000 men with this message and have them commit to the challenge."

Oh man, now I know I'm crazy! Who is going to listen to a wacko like me ask them to be a part of a movement to see one million men join together to impart God's blessing to the next generation?

The night was quiet and the presence of God was strong, making going back to sleep impossible. Who would want to join me? I was so wound up with this new aspect of the vision that I decided to check out Amazon to see what I could find related to what I was experiencing. I had no idea what to look for or what I would find. I typed into the search box the word *Blessing*. The first book that came up was, *The Blessing*,[2] by John Trent and Gary Smalley. I was not familiar with the book, only with the names of the authors.

To my discredit, they always seemed a bit touchy-feely for me, so I had never read any of their books before. As I skimmed the pages, I began to get excited to see that so many of the things the Lord was showing me were

---

[2]Smalley, G., & Trent, J. (1986). *The Blessing.* Nashville, TN: Thomas Nelson.

already in print right before my eyes. It was confirmation for me. If God is doing something significant, He will be doing it in many places, using many different people. As excited as I was, however, the idea of reaching one million patriarchs who would make a

commitment to participate in this vision seemed outlandish. I continued to scan through the rest of the book and what I discovered next totally blew me away. The authors were presenting the exact same vision to their readers: 1,000,000 family leaders speaking blessing into the lives of the next and youngest generation. I was awestruck and couldn't believe what I was reading.

At this point, I was convinced. These midnight promptings I had received WERE from the Lord. The challenge before me was immense, but now I was certain that God had spoken to me. I knew it was going to turn into a lifetime journey. What a humbling and exciting privilege to be a part of something God wants to do across the earth.

The **Grampa's Time ministry** exists to **Enlist, Equip, Encourage, and Empower 1,000,000 Grandfathers and Fathers to Lay Hands on their Grandchildren and Children, Speaking the Blessing of God into Their Lives.**

It's Your Turn

Grampa Ellerby had no idea. He faithfully and passionately served and loved Jesus. He was the conduit of blessing for my generation. His faithfulness contributed to God's work in my life—it is the way the divine family structure is designed to work. As my family patriarch, J.W. Ellerby fulfilled his mandate. Now it's my turn. It is my responsibility that my grandchildren be the recipients of God's blessing through my commitment as the family patriarch in their lives.

It is also your turn.

I am convinced that the earth is on the brink of a major move of God, and I believe that as God restores His divine structure in the family, we will see an awakening in the youngest generation alive today that has never been witnessed before. My conviction is that *where sin abounds, grace does much more abound*. No matter how dark the times, Jesus will never be defeated.

The remainder of this book is designed to present a practical plan for men like you and me to participate in what God is doing all over the earth to re-establish His glory among the nations. It's our time.

IT'S GRAMPA'S TIME !

The 5 Step Blueprint

Chapter 2

"There is only one thing stronger than all the armies of the world: and that is an idea whose time has come."

Victor Hugo

EVERY GREAT ACCOMPLISHMENT, CAPTIVATING STORY, AWE-INSPIRING structure or building starts with the same thing—an idea. When that idea begins to take on life, it requires articulation and a blueprint. Without a blueprint, it is impossible for others to participate in the building of the idea.

I have been involved in the construction of many buildings over the years. The first house my wife and I built, we, like anyone else, started with a dream to own our own home. We began by looking at pictures of houses we would like to have and sorted them according to size and design. The first step was to find out if we could even afford to buy one. Being newbies at the game, we didn't have a clear understanding of how to proceed with convincing a bank to give us the money for construction. We calculated that we could afford X amount for a monthly payment and speculated what that amount of money would allow us to build. Still only guessing, we concocted a strategy to present to the lender.

From all of the pictures we looked at, we selected three we liked, starting from the largest to the smallest. From there, I painstakingly collected quotes from different trades, priced out materials down to the penny, and added in whatever contingency I thought would be necessary. Our plan was to go to the lending institution with the picture of the largest home, along with all of my calculations, and do our best to submit as rosy a presentation as possible, to win over the banker. We would begin with the largest house and work our way down to the smallest of the three, if necessary.

Everyone needed a picture ... so they knew exactly what they were building

To our amazement, the lender approved our financing on the first try. We were ecstatic. The first request from the bank after approval was, "Do you have a blueprint available?" Since I had purchased three copies of blueprints for each house, I proudly handed one over; he required two.

From there I went to the town hall for the necessary permits. They required three sets of blueprints ... then the excavator, the lumber supplier, the plumber, the electrician, the tin basher, the window manufacturer, the truss company, etc., etc. Everyone wanted a copy of the blueprints. Everyone needed a picture of the house so they knew exactly what they were constructing. It's many years ago, but I think I provided over a dozen copies of blueprints to different people involved in the construction process.

Everyone was singing from the same songbook—everyone was on the same page. In order to build a proper building, reading from the same page is required.

God's Patriarchal Blueprint

In my pursuit to understand what God was saying to me about the patriarch's role in passing the blessing of God on to the next generation, I wanted to have a biblical picture of what that impartation was going to look like. I needed a blueprint. I had an idea, and I believed that idea was the prompting of God's Spirit, but I needed more. I needed a picture.

I began a diligent search of the Scriptures to see what the Bible had to say about patriarchs and grandfathers. I came across Genesis 48, and it was like the Holy Spirit said to me,

"This is it. This is your blueprint."

As I read through the chapter, I was mesmerized by the imagery I could see in the story. It was like I became a part of it—as though it was me and my grandfather. I was energized and eager to share the blueprint with the world. It was time to start building.

I'll explore Genesis 48 in more detail later, but I would like to submit an overview here to give us some context for the blueprint.

The Genesis 48 Story

Some time later Joseph was told, "Your father is ill." So he took his two sons Manasseh and Ephraim along with him. When Jacob was told, "Your son Joseph has come to you," <u>Israel rallied his strength and sat up on the bed.</u> Jacob said to Joseph, "God Almighty appeared to me at Luz in the land of Canaan, and there he blessed me and said to me, `I am going to make you fruitful and increase your numbers. I will make you a community of peoples, and I will give this land as an everlasting possession <u>to your descendants after you.</u>' .... When Israel saw the sons of Joseph, he asked, "Who are these?" "They are the sons God has given me here," Joseph said to his father. Then Israel said, "<u>Bring them to me so I may bless them.</u>" Now Israel's eyes were failing because of old age, and he could hardly see. So Joseph brought his sons close to him, and his father kissed them and embraced them. Israel said to Joseph, "I never expected to see your face again, and now God has allowed me to see your children too." Then Joseph removed them from Israel's knees and bowed down with his face to the ground. And Joseph took both of them .... Then he blessed Joseph and said, "May the God before whom my fathers Abraham and Isaac walked faithfully, the God who has been my shepherd all my life to this day, the Angel who has delivered me from all harm—<u>may he bless these boys.</u> May they be called by my name and the names of my fathers Abraham and Isaac, and may they increase greatly on the earth."

Genesis 48:1-16

There are portions of this Scripture that require further study at another time, but for the purpose of our study regarding the basic blueprint, I included the scene as the Bible records it.

Joseph was the second most powerful man in all the world. I imagine him as a man of great power and wisdom; a man of significant stature. He was charming, handsome, well-groomed, and a presence among the people. I am sure his self-confidence was clearly evident and his position and wealth were obvious to all onlookers. There was nothing he could not provide for his family—something like the Donald Trump of his time. Even though there was a devastating famine in the land, you know his family did not go without.

He was an impressive man. There is something about Joseph I find immensely intriguing. It is apparent that his position and his power did not diminish his ability to understand and long for a broader knowledge of the God of his roots and an experience with the God of his father and his forefathers. Even though he was deeply entrenched in the Egyptian culture and politics, Joseph had not lost his awareness of God's leadership and covering in his life.

The part of the story I find most riveting is Joseph's realization that his father, Jacob, had something nobody else could provide for either him or his children. Ephraim and Manasseh were about to experience something that they had no idea of the impact it would make on their lives. Joseph obviously knew something and recognized its value for his family. He further understood that if his dad died before he had secured that particular something, both he and his children would miss out on a desired level of favor throughout their lives. What was that something? It was GOD'S BLESSING.

I surmise the conversation between Joseph and his boys to have gone something like this:

Joseph: Boys, we are going out to the farm to see Grampa Jacob.

Boys: Aw, do we have to? We were planning to go to the camel races.

Joseph: No camel races today. Get your things and get in the slave-carried rickshaw. Grampa's not well, and we need to go see him before it's too late.

Boys: Oh, alright. At least Grampa usually has beef jerky.

They were kids and I'm sure were not fully aware of the importance of what was actually taking place, not unlike our own families, who may not comprehend what grampa is up to when he lays hands on them and prays for them. Regardless of whether they understand or not, this is about our responsibility before God to fulfill our appointed patriarchal role.

When Joseph and his sons arrived at his father's place, Joseph initiated a ritual that he clearly understood to be critical to his family's future. Joseph told his father that he had brought his two sons with him for Jacob to lay hands on them and to speak God's blessing into their lives.

The story goes that Jacob rallied his strength to get off his deathbed and called the boys to himself. He then laid his hands on the boys and prayed a blessing over Joseph and his sons. Both Jacob and Joseph clearly understood Jacob's patriarchal role in the family. They both understood the authority associated with laying hands on another person, and they recognized the directive power of the words spoken.

What we see in this story is a blueprint. It is the picture we are looking for.

From this portion of Scripture, the **'5 Step Blueprint'** is formulated. That which Jacob demonstrated with Joseph and his children is the same process you and I as family patriarchs should model in the lives of our children and grandchildren.

Step 1–YOU are the PATRIARCH

Do not underestimate your place in your family tree. Headship is essential to God's divine family structure. The role of the patriarch in the Bible was one of **leadership**, **stewardship**, and most importantly—**covering** (Genesis 48:8-16).

Do not believe the lie that you no longer play a very important role in your family. That is not true. More than ever, our families need us. The patriarch does not necessarily have direct influence in the lives of the generations that follow, but they do provide spiritual covering and blessing. Throughout the Old and New Testaments, the patriarchs imparted blessings to their children and grandchildren. The fruit of those blessings often took many years to be fulfilled, but typically, evidence shows they were fulfilled.

It is my conviction that the greatest thing we can do to help shape the lives and the future of the generations that will follow us is to impart God's blessing upon them and then stand in faith together, knowing that God is faithful and He will raise strong men and women of God to change the course of our needy world.

Step 2–The BLESSING

The purpose of the Blessing was to transfer or impart the divine covering of God over the recipient and to set the course for their lives. The concept of the blessing is used in the Bible over six hundred times. The word *Blessing* literally means to **Invoke God for the purpose of prospering.** Not every blessing recorded in the Scriptures was meant for the same purpose. However, the blessings which are recorded typically focus on one or more of the following aspects or common denominators indicating the heart of God and the intent of the patriarch.

1.	The <u>KNOWLEDGE</u> of God	Ephesians 1:3-14
2.	The <u>POWER</u> of God	1 Chronicles 29:11 ; Acts 1:8
3.	The <u>FAVOR</u> of God	3 John 2; Psalm 5:11-12
4.	The <u>PURPOSE</u> of God	Romans 1:1; Matthew 9:37-38
5.	The <u>DESIGN</u> of God	Psalm 139: 13-16; John 1:40-41

I believe that when we pray for our families, we should impart all five aspects, together or individually, as appropriate times and circumstances dictate. They should be a continual focus of our commitment to our families, to see the Spirit of Christ released INTO their lives, and to be a part of setting direction FOR their lives.

Step 3–<u>Laying on of Hands</u>

The concept of laying hands on someone and praying the blessing on them goes all the way back to the book of Genesis and the blessing Isaac passed on to Jacob.

Jesus insisted that children were never to be prevented from coming to Him and when they did come, the Bible says, **"And he took the children in his arms, placed his hands on them and blessed them"** (Mark 10:16).

1 Timothy 4:14 indicates that the laying on of hands was a common part of the church for the releasing of ministry in the body of Christ.

There is something powerful that happens when we "lay hands on" someone for the purpose of imparting God's blessing into their lives.

Step 4–The Spoken Word

The Apostle James indicated that the tongue is like the rudder of a ship, which can direct the entire vessel (James 3:4). Proverbs 19:21 declares that **"death and life are in the power of the tongue"** (NAS). It is with words that we can ignite dynamic life into the lives of our grandchildren and children. It is with words that we can significantly encourage and support the awakening of God's Spirit in them.

The Apostle Paul stated that **"Faith comes by HEARING ... the word of Christ"** (Romans 10:17 NAS). Speaking words of blessing over our grandchildren and children, therefore, becomes an extremely valuable exercise for us as grandfathers and fathers.

Step 5–Faith

The fifth component of the impartation is **BELIEVING** that laying our hands on our children and grandchildren, and then speaking words of blessing into their lives will, in fact, release something in the Spirit within them. Everything in God's Kingdom is activated by faith. Faith is the **"substance of things hoped for, the evidence of things not seen"** (Hebrews 11:1 NKJV).

We can't always see what is going on with the work of God and truthfully, many of us will not be alive when the full work of the Holy Spirit in our family members' lives becomes fully evident. If we think there is nothing happening in their lives just because we don't initially see the fruit, then we are not living by faith. There is much going on in the unseen, spiritual realm that is powerful and positive.

As Winston Churchill said, "Never, never, never give up." Faith is the energy. Faith is the power that keeps us motivated and confident that God will *complete that which He started* (Philippians 1:6).

That is our blueprint. God wants to change the world, and men, he wants to use *you*. This is a major part of His plan. The re-engagement of the patriarchs of families laying hands on their grandchildren and children while speaking the Word of the Lord in faith into their lives will change the course of history.

Men of God, your families, your communities, your churches, and our nations need you more than ever. We now have the framework, a picture, and a blueprint from which to build. God has a plan. All that is required is for you and me to join the journey and be a part of what the Lord is doing all over the world. It's our time. It's Grampa's time.

This is the most significant contribution we will ever make to our family. We may or may not see in our lifetime all the fruit of this blessing, however, we must be convinced that the entire world will eventually witness a powerful demonstration of God's work in their lives.

Impart the Blessing

This Blessing was intended to be passed on to generation after generation through the faithful commitment and prayer of the previous generation. The Apostle Paul indicates that we are *Body, Soul,* and *Spirit* and that each part of us must be influenced by the Lord as we seek to serve Him. The impartation, therefore, is passed on by the *Laying on of Hands* (the body), through the *Spoken Word* (the soul) and activated by *Faith* (the Spirit).

GENERATIONAL ROOTS

Chapter 3

―――――――――――◄◆►―――――――――――

"If the family were a fruit, it would be an orange,
a circle of sections, held together but separable—
each segment distinct."
Letty Cottin Pogrebin

―――――――――――◄◆►―――――――――――

➤ "Like father, like son."

➤ "An apple doesn't fall far from the tree."

➤ His father is a plumber—the son is a plumber.

➤ Her mother is a musician—the daughter plays the piano.

➤ The uncle struggles with gambling—both his sons and his nephew already visit the casinos.

➤ Grampa wouldn't "darken the door" of a church—the grandchildren view church as "religious junk."

➤ His grandfather and great-great-grandfather were ministers and now he is a minister.

It's obvious there are patterns that are repeated over and over again inside the fabric and framework of families. It's interesting how these patterns seem to run for generations. We have all witnessed how, for example, if an individual is a plumber, there is a high possibility that his son may become a plumber. Or, if a woman loves music, her children may, in fact, become musicians. If you go a level deeper inside of a family tree, you can often find similarities that are even more profound: things such as attitudes, body movements, personal convictions, or even perspectives on life matters.

Inside of the family gene pool it's not uncommon to associate family members based on their physical resemblances—same eyes, same height and body shape, dark hair, light hair, noses, etc. It's comical how the first words you hear out of the mouth of curious onlookers when a baby is born, are, "Oh, I think she looks just like …" or "he definitely has his mother's eyes … or her father's nose …"

My wife once pointed out that she could see some of my family features in a photograph of my great-great-grandfather that was taken in the early 1800's.

We also share qualities in our emotional and/or mental perspectives, such as quiet demeanor, aggressive disposition, loud voices, compassionate verses, more insensitive, and on and on the comparisons go. I may have even heard it said when one of my children was misbehaving, "You act just like your father." Imagine! Don't laugh; it's possible that you may have heard something similar yourself at one time.

I am in no way a psychologist, nor do I have any training in sociology or psychology. I am, however, fascinated that God has created us in such a way that we, as family members, are linked together with one another in far deeper ways than most understand or appreciate. The Apostle Paul indicates in 1 Thessalonians 5:23 that we are to keep our whole **"spirit, soul, and body** blameless at the coming of our Lord Jesus Christ." These distinctions indicate that we are far more than only physical or social creatures. We are made up of body, soul, **and** spirit.

This is the Mystery of our Tri-part Being. How are we Connected Spiritually?

I referred earlier to my great-great-grandfather. His name was James Blackett Ellerby. He was born in 1748. He penned the following letter to members of his family on January 1st, 1807.

"It would give me unspeakable pleasure could I hear of you and all my dear brothers and sisters walking in the way of heaven. But I am at a loss what to say to you on the subject because I have wrote to you so frequently on this important subject. I have just been looking for that text with a design to preach from it this evening. "This year thou shalt die". Perhaps before the close of this year on which we have just entered you and I will be numbered with the dead, then let us be ready for in such an hour as we think no the son of man cometh. O repent of your sins turn to God with all your heart and you may receive an inheritance among them that are sanctified by faith that is in Jesus Christ."

As sure as you are living now upon earth you will seriously think of my exhortations. O that you may think of them before it is too late! Now whatsoever your hand findeth to do do it with all your might for there is no repentance nor knowledge nor device in the grave whither you are going. Nothing in the world would give me greater happiness and satisfaction of mind than to hear of and see my dear brother and sister enquiring their way to Zion with their faces thitherward. Never will you, depend upon it, be happy till you forsake sin and turn to God with all your heart and soul. Now begin to live for God and heaven and cast this world and sin behind. But what am I doing I despair of ... unless God opens your eyes: therefore, I will bow my knees to the Father of our Lord Jesus Christ of whom the whole family in heaven and earth is named and lift up my heart to His throne in fervent prayer for you that you may be saved."

Please give my kindest love to your children my nephews and nieces and to all my brothers and sisters, Christn Richards and all my brethren and sisters in the gospel of Jesus Christ. Give my kind love to the preachers and particularly Mr. Gibbons.""

I remain your affectionate brother Jas Blackett Ellerby"

Did my great-great-grandfather's encounter with Jesus actually have a bearing on my personal journey? What was his experience? I'm curious to know what he looked like, how he thought, and what interested him, but more importantly, I want to understand his faith.

The part I find most captivating about James Blackett Ellerby is that he was a circuit preacher in England in the 1700 and 1800's. He lived in tough times. There were respectable tradesmen, workers, and street sellers, but there were also hordes of poor and destitute people who seldom had regular work, but lived as best they could. Petty and violent crimes were common in his day and consequences for those crimes were meted out harshly.

According to Dr. Matthew White,[3] "rioting was a familiar feature of daily life in both towns and the countryside, and many people came to fear the power of the 'mob'. Crowd action was particularly strong in London, where people regularly threw stones at the carriages of leading politicians or booed unpopular ministers. In 1780, after the government had passed legislation giving more political rights to Catholics, thousands of people rioted for a week in London in protest. Catholics were attacked, and Catholic property smashed up. All of London's major prisons were burnt to the ground and the Bank of England came under attack. The incident became known as the Gordon Riots."

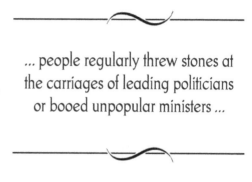

... people regularly threw stones at the carriages of leading politicians or booed unpopular ministers ...

Tim Lambert explains how "the early 18th century was noted for its lack of religious enthusiasm and the churches in England lacked vigor. In the mid-18th century, however, things began to change. In 1739 the great evangelists George Whitefield and John Wesley began preaching the gospel throughout the country. Wesley eventually created a new religious movement called the Methodists. In Wales, there was a great revival in the years 1738-1742. Scotland was also swept by revival in the mid-18th century."[4]

It was in this environment that James Blackett Ellerby was born. It was on the coattails of that move of God that he traveled around the nation

[3] White, M. (October 14, 2009). Popular Politics in the 18th Century. *The British Library, Georgian Britain*. Retrieved from https://www.bl.uk/georgian-britain/articles/popular-politics-in-the-18th-century

[4] Lambert, T. A History of Religion in 18th Century England. *A World History Encyclopedia*. Retrieved from http://www.localhistories.org/18thcenturyxian.html

preaching the gospel and challenging people to give their lives to Jesus and to walk in a manner worthy of His Lordship. His conviction is obvious. His passion was pure and his experience and transformed life undeniable. He had met Jesus and knew that his family needed to know Him as well.

I can only assume that my great-great-grandfather had been significantly influenced by the likes of Whitefield and Wesley, but I am also of the mind that he probably wasn't the first in the family tree who was a believer and an advocate of embracing Jesus as their Savior.

The correlation between my great-great-grampa Ellerby and those that have followed him is very intriguing to me. Look at the following chart:

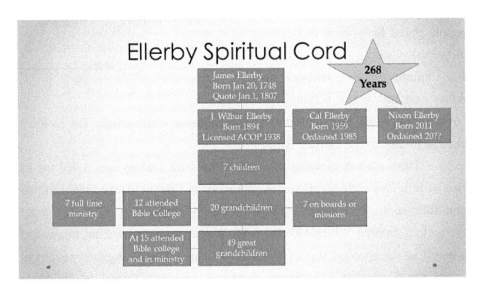

There are many gaps of which I do not have record, but what I do have shows a consistent and common theme. Great-great-Grampa Ellerby was a preacher in the 1700 and 1800's. My grandfather Wilbur Ellerby became a licensed minister in 1938, and I was ordained a minister in 1985. Through my Grampa Wilbur's seven children there came twenty grandchildren, seven of whom have served in full-time ministry. Of those twenty grandchildren came forty-nine great-grandchildren, fifteen of whom have attended Bible college, with many of those going on to serve in full-time ministry.

Something that took place in the life of my great-great-grandfather, James Blackett Ellerby, has found its way down through the ages to me and my generation, all these years later. He was the patriarch of family members who love Jesus and have sought to serve Him for many generations.

This phenomenon is much more than an emotional, social, or cultural occurrence. It goes far deeper than psychological or sociological patterns. The manifest power of God has been witnessed in the hearts of many generations of my family. The individual relevance of a personal spiritual awakening has been repeated over and over again in the lives of these family members. Each one has had their own unique story and encounter with Christ, but each had arrived at the same spot at the foot of the cross with the eyes of their heart opened and embracing the redemptive work of Jesus. Each one of my siblings, cousins, aunts, and uncles that profess their love for Jesus is a living testimony of the power of great-great-grampa's prayer and blessing.

"Now begin to live for God and heaven and cast this world and sin behind. But what am I doing I despair of ... unless God opens your eyes: therefore, I will bow my knees to the Father of our Lord Jesus Christ of whom the whole family in heaven and earth is named and lift up my heart to His throne in fervent prayer for you that you may be saved."

This was the prayer that was prayed over 250 years ago.

What Does The Bible Say About Generational Foundations?

> "I call heaven and earth to witness against you today, that I have set before you life and death, blessing and curse. Therefore choose life, that you and your offspring may live ..."
> Deuteronomy 30:19 (ESV)

When Moses assembled the children of Israel together to present to them the covenant God was making with them, it was clear this covenant was never intended to be a short-term, one-generational promise. I love the way the instructions are laid out. God said to Moses, "I'm giving you an option here."

1 – Deuteronomy 30:19

1) **"I have set before you ..."** Here are your choices. Follow Me and worship Me ... or don't.
2) **"Therefore choose life ... "** Make the right choice.
3) **"So that you AND your offspring may live ..."**

It was clear from God's promises that the next generations were very much included in the covenant. The onus on the people was that the choice they were going to make that day was going to be carried on for generations to come. God was declaring that this decision was not to be made lightly because their children and their grandchildren would be profoundly impacted by their choice.

2 – The Second of the 10 Commandments

"You shall not bow down to them or worship them; for I, the LORD your God, am a jealous God, punishing the children for the sin of the parents to the third and fourth generation of those who hate me, **but showing love to a thousand generations of those who love me** and keep my commandments" (Exodus 20:5-6).

The principle was clear for the children of Israel. If you worship other gods, your family, to the third and fourth generations, will suffer the consequences. But if you will have a heart for God, then a thousand generations of your family tree will experience His blessings.

There is clearly a generational cord, a connection that ties the family together, making it one living organism.

3 – David Spoke Prophetically

"But the lovingkindness of the LORD is from everlasting to everlasting on those who fear Him, And **His righteousness to children's children** …" (Psalm 103:17 NAS).

"Praise the LORD! How blessed is the man who fears the LORD, Who greatly delights in His commandments. **His descendants will be mighty on earth**; The generation of the upright will be blessed," (Psalm 112:1-2 NAS).

4 – The Blessing of Abraham

"Abram fell facedown, and God said to him, "As for me, this is my covenant with you: You will be the father of many nations. No longer will you be called Abram; your name will be Abraham, for I have made you a father of many nations. I will make you very fruitful; I will make nations of you, and kings will come from you. I will establish my covenant as an everlasting covenant **between me and you and your descendants after you for the generations to come, to be your God and the God of your descendants after you**. The whole land of Canaan, where you now reside as a foreigner, **I will give as an everlasting possession to you and your descendants after you; and I will be their God**" (Gen. 17:3-8).

Without getting into the theology of the blessing of Abraham, let me say this. The foundation of our Christian faith is rooted in these promises. God was teaching Abraham that because of his faith, the whole of mankind was going to be given the opportunity to enter into the fulness of God's plan for humanity.

> Abraham was God's appointed servant

It is this very chapter of the Bible that reveals that God sees every generation at once. God sees the whole picture. We see linear; God sees complete. God not only saw Abraham, He saw you and me. Abraham was God's appointed servant to be "the guy." It was God's design to enlarge His connectedness with the rest of humanity for generations to eternity, by hand-picking Abraham to be the Father of faith. And because of Abraham's obedience, trust, and commitment to God's leading, salvation by faith alone became a reality.

Abraham was the "Father of Faith," the patriarch, the one appointed as the "head" of the family tree. He was linked to many, many generations that would follow him. His actions for that day were going to set the course and lay out the necessary framework for not only his children but every one of his descendants.

5 – New Testament Blessings of Abraham

"Yet he did not waver through unbelief regarding the promise of God, but was strengthened in his faith and gave glory to God, being fully persuaded that God had power to do what he had promised. This is why "it was credited to him as righteousness." The words "it was credited to him" **were written not for him alone, but also for us**, to whom God will credit righteousness— for us who believe in him who raised Jesus our Lord from the dead. He was delivered over to death for our sins and was raised to life for our justification" (Romans 4:20-25).

Paul unveils a wonderful truth here in Romans: The words, "it was credited to him" **were written not for him alone, but also for us …**" tell us that the words were not recorded only for Abraham's benefit, but that in His *all knowing, all wise foresight,* God was completing the bond between Himself and those who would come to Him in faith, as Abraham did.

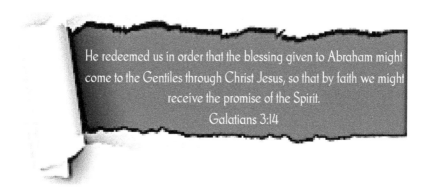

He redeemed us in order that the blessing given to Abraham might come to the Gentiles through Christ Jesus, so that by faith we might receive the promise of the Spirit.
Galatians 3:14

It's Your Time

Grampa. It's your time. Imagine 200 years from today. What part are you going to play in establishing the experiences with Jesus of your great-great-grandchildren and beyond?

I cannot overstate the importance for men of God to capture the vision and urgency to embrace their responsibility to be the disseminators of God's blessing on their descendants. James Blackett Ellerby could not have known what the generations after him would look like. He has been, however, an integral player in the journey of people like me. He fulfilled his appointed placement by honoring the Lord Jesus with his life and has passed on God's blessing so that I could personally experience Christ in a most profound way.

Thanks, Grampa.

WHY is the FAMILY SO IMPORTANT?

Chapter 4

"There are no ordinary people. You have never talked to a mere mortal. Nations, cultures, arts, civilizations – these are mortal, and their life is to ours as the life of a gnat. But it is immortals whom we joke with, work with, marry, snub, and exploit."

C. S. Lewis

THE JEWISH CULTURE IS A RICH CULTURE, AND THE JEWISH FAITH HAS developed magnificent symbolism and imagery associated with the Scriptures. As westernized Christians, we often miss or even misrepresent the meaning of certain passages of the Bible either because we don't know or don't fully understand the context in which the passage was written. When we read the Scriptures, we generally interpret them based on our own western filters and our own understanding of English words that don't completely project the full intention of the author. We too often lack, or at least don't fully comprehend, the geographical settings, the middle eastern *ethos,* and the history in which the texts were written.

One significant example of this is the meaning and understanding that the Jewish culture has when defining the concept of blessing. As westerners, we have limited or confined the definition of blessings to mean one of three rather simplistic thoughts:

1. Happiness
2. Favor/provision
3. Thanksgiving

While each of these thoughts contributes to a partial understanding, there is a deeper intent associated with the term.

When the Jewish people express blessing, they are declaring their admiration for the Spirit of God, who is enveloped in every aspect of the object of blessing. They are expressing their awareness of the intricacy with which God has represented Himself in that specific part of creation. It defines the reality that God wants to be seen at every level of our lives.

'For in Him we live and move and have our being.'
Acts 17:28

Daniella Levy[5] writes a blog that gives us a little richer insight and clarification on this subject.

---

[5] Daniella Levy, Crash Course in Jewish Blessings. Retrieved from http://www.aish.com/jl/jewish-law/blessings/Crash-Course-in-Jewish-Blessings.html

... first things first: what does the word "bless" mean, anyway? In Hebrew, the root that means "bless" is b.r.kh, and the Sages explain that it means "to increase" or "bring down Divine abundance." When I "bless" you, I am asking God to increase your health, wealth, happiness or whatever it may be, to shine His light on you... in essence, to give you more of Himself. So what could it possibly mean for me to "bless" God for creating the apple I'm about to eat?

The key to understanding this is to recognize the purpose of these blessings. It is not merely to show gratitude.
<u>The purpose of a blessing is awareness.</u>

When I hold an apple in my hand and say, "Blessed are You, Lord, our God, King of the Universe, who creates the fruit of the tree," what I'm really saying is a lot more than just "thanks for making this apple." I'm saying, "Your presence in this world has been made that much greater, has increased, through this fruit You created that I am about to enjoy."

<u>I'm declaring that whatever it is I'm making the blessing for</u> – whether it's a food I'm enjoying, a roll of thunder I heard, or a mitzvah I'm about to perform – <u>is increasing God's presence in the world, through my recognition of His role in creating or commanding it.</u>

This is one of the main themes of Judaism: <u>channeling the Divine into the mundane and revealing the spiritual through the physical.</u> Through this worldly experience, I experience God; and when I declare that recognition, I make His presence in the world that much more known.

<u>Simply put: in this apple, I see God.</u>

When we bless something, or more specifically, *someone*, we are, in fact, expressing our admiration for God as the Creator of that specific thing or special person. People, the apex of God's creation, are understood to be even that much more valuable. They are not only the image of God but vessels housing the Spirit of God. That being said, when we bless our grandchildren and children, we are literally acknowledging God's masterpiece within them.

Therefore, there is a far more profound reality that associates family members to one another. It is an unseen reality. It is a spiritual reality. It is

… Christ in me, the hope of glory.

"So God created mankind in his own image, in the image of God he created them; male and female he created them" (Genesis 1:27).

What does this Scripture teach us? We not only share the DNA of our parents and ancestors, but we literally have the DNA of God woven into us. It is this very element of our existence that separates humanity from the rest of creation. We are the *IMAGO DEI.* "The Image of God."

We are the Image of God. The Imago Dei

"Then the LORD God formed a man from the dust of the ground and breathed into his nostrils the breath of life, and the man became a living being" (Genesis 2:7).

We breathe the very breath of God. No other part of creation has the breath of God emanating from their being. The angels marvel and the demons tremble at the beauty and majesty of God's most magnificent creature.

The Family is a Divine Living Entity

If man as an individual is the image of God, then it provokes further thought regarding the family unit as a collection of individuals bearing that image.

What is the significance of the family? Why is it so important?

The LORD God said, "It is not good for the man to be alone. I will make a helper suitable for him ..." But for Adam no suitable helper was found. So the LORD God caused the man to fall into a deep sleep; and while he was sleeping, he took one of the man's ribs and then closed up the place with flesh. Then the LORD God made a woman from the rib he had taken out of the man, and he brought her to the man. The man said, "This is now bone of my bones and flesh of my flesh; she shall be called 'woman,' for she was taken out of man." That is why a man leaves his father and mother and is united to his wife, and they become one flesh.

Genesis 2:18,20-24

Forgive me as I digress, but I must tell you that I identify with this verse. When I first saw my (now) wife, my immediate thought was, in fact, "WHOA ... MAN! It's not good for me to be alone. I need one of those. Actually, I need THAT one." And subsequently, less than a year later, we were married and have enjoyed the pleasure of one another's partnership for the last thirty-five years. God comes up with some great ideas.

Ok, back to the family.

It was God who created the family by creating Eve for Adam and then gave them strict instructions to be "fruitful and multiply." Unless things have changed since then, I think Adam thought that was a wonderful idea.

The family—a precious foundation to all of God's intentions

The relationship with God was set on a replicable trajectory. God's plan was now in full motion. Humans would continually reproduce and continually introduce more and more God-breathed creatures into the world, allowing this wondrous union between God and His beloved creation to stimulate joy and intimacy in a very beautiful way.

THE FAMILY!
It is a Precious Foundation to all of God's Intentions

The assembly of His masterpiece and the infusion of His Spirit portray to all of creation the splendor of His ultimate craftsmanship—humanity. His fingerprints ON them and His breath IN them; that is what makes us different. That is what makes us precious in His sight. That is the mystery of all His creation. That is what necessitates redemption.

In his paper, *Family: More Than a Cultural Phenomenon,* Rev. F. Stanley Keehlwetter[6] wrote, "The traditional family unit, therefore, is more than the consequence of evolutionary social interaction or merely a cultural phenomenon. **It is a spiritual entity, designed by God, with intrinsic value and purpose.**"

I love Dr. Keehlwetter's statement that the family was *designed* by God. He had to have a system. He had to have a plan. No other part of creation had the same elements bestowed upon it. To see this and understand it is to recognize the immense value Almighty God places on the family unit.

---

[6] Keehlwetter, S. *Family: More Than a Cultural Phenomenon.* Retrieved from http://visionandvalues.org/docs/familymatters/Keehlwetter_Stan.pdf

"The God who made the world and everything in it is the Lord of heaven and earth and does not live in temples built by human hands. And he is not served by human hands, as if he needed anything. Rather, <u>he himself gives everyone life and breath and everything else</u>. From one man he made all the nations, that they should inhabit the whole earth; and he marked out their appointed times in history and the boundaries of their lands. <u>God did this so that they would seek him and perhaps reach out for him and find him</u>, though he is not far from any one of us. '<u>For in him we live and move and have our being</u>.' As some of your own poets have said, 'We are his offspring.' "<u>Therefore since we are God's offspring, we should not think that the divine being</u> is like gold or silver or stone—an image made by human design and skill.

Acts 17:24-29

Paul clearly proclaimed to the people of Athens that there was something profoundly special about humanity, making it entirely unique from anything else in existence. Even though God created everything in the world, only human beings and the family unit are living organisms in the divine sense. God Himself gives everyone **"life and breath and everything else."**

People, and families for that matter, are designed to function as one unit and to be sustained by an intimate relationship with their Creator. The assembled groupings of human beings, otherwise known as the family, are quite literally, living, breathing, divine organisms.

Here's What we Know About a Living Organism:

A living organism is made up of a multitude of individual, yet connected cells and molecules. Each of those cells share the same DNA and is designed to live attached to the rest of the body. Each part is to contribute to the strength and life of the whole.

1. **THIS COLLECTION OF CELLS IS SUSTAINED BY THE SAME SOURCE.** In the case of the family, it is sustained by the very breath of God. There is a spiritual cord tying one generation to the other. God has put His life into the family connection. It needs the breath of God to remain healthy and alive.

2. **THE BODY IS DESIGNED TO NURTURE AND CARE FOR ITSELF.** The body embraces all other cells that share the same DNA. Every cell supports the others. It is a marvelous example of how love and acceptance are so vital to the overall well-being of a family.

3. **THE BODY IS DESIGNED TO PROTECT AND HEAL ITSELF.** When one element or cell is wounded, the body is designed to fight off the enemy and preserve the health of the wounded member. Without this component, the body will ultimately become sick and

die. When a family member is wounded, the rest of the family is affected and needs to come to the aid of the wounded member.

> The family unit is a living organism in the divine sense

4. **THE BODY IS DESIGNED TO REPLENISH ITSELF.** The necessary elements of nutrition, exercise, and proper environment all contribute to the ongoing energy and replenishment that the body requires. The absorption of nutrients, natural vitamins, and sustenance are reminders of how the family requires ongoing investments of love, encouragement, enjoyment, and fellowship.

5. **THE BODY IS DESIGNED TO REPRODUCE ITSELF.** The physical body sheds some 600,000 cells a day and reproduces new cells to replace those, every minute of every day. The family is continually cycling through members. The generations that pass on are replaced with new descendants that are entering this world to further expand the lineage and presence of the family and its name. Each one is connected to the previous and the next. The transference of God's blessing from one generation is not just a nice social tradition. It is God's plan for making sure that every generation experiences His love and communion.

I've always found it curious that when the Old Testament patriarchs passed a blessing on to the next generation, they often prayed that the recipient of the blessing would have families as plentiful as the stars of the sky and the sand of the sea. Not until I realized that the family was a part of God's divine strategy, did I understand how important this truth really is. It has always been His intention that the spiritual cord that houses His own spiritual DNA not be broken but be carried on from one generation to the next. He longs to express His love and His nature to every human ever born, and His chosen pathway for doing that is through the family unit. He created families in such a way that the individuals of one generation might benefit from the faithfulness and commitment to God by each preceding generation.

The Apostle Paul stated in Acts 17:27 that **"God did this so that they would seek him and perhaps reach out for him and find him …"**

As members of one another at our very core, we begin to recognize the degree of our divine nature and eternal intent for relationships. Seeing the family as God sees it, will help us to appreciate more fully the role we play as patriarchs. It will help us to see why we must be engaged in God's plan. It will also help us to understand that every generation plays an important part in the lives and experiences of the generations that come after us. It makes David's impassioned prayer of Psalm 71:18 make greater sense. **"Even when I am old and gray, do not forsake me, my God, till I declare your power to the next generation, your mighty acts to all who are to come."**

Pass It On

Grandfathers, as the patriarch of your family, God has placed and appointed you as a catalyst in this masterfully designed and crafted structure. You may not always have the privilege, due to circumstances beyond your control, to directly shape and influence the lives of your grandchildren, but you are still God's choice for the spiritual connection and life in their journey to and with Him. The life of Christ will be exponentially enhanced through the involvement and contribution of *Grampa*. This is the way the spiritual DNA intertwines throughout the living organism known as *the family*. As you exercise your responsibility of passing on the blessing of God to the next generation, you will be fulfilling the divine mandate bestowed on you by a God who has chosen to be reflected in the world through His most treasured creation. You got it—YOUR FAMILY!

THE PRINCIPLE of HEADSHIP

Chapter 5

"… although He existed in the form of God, did not
regard equality with God a thing to be grasped, but
emptied Himself, taking the form of a bond-servant,
and being made in the likeness of men. Being
found in appearance as a man, He humbled
Himself by becoming obedient to the point
of death, even death on a cross."
Philippians 2:6-8 (NAS)

AS A KID, I REMEMBER HEARING A STORY THAT HAS NEVER LEFT ME. THE story goes that in the early 1930's there was a farmer who, like most, was doing his best to survive the dusty, drought-plagued "Dirty 30's." It was a very difficult time and he did whatever he had to do in order to provide for his wife and five children. The ground was parched from lack of rain and the livestock were thin because the normally rich and lush pasture land was now brown and dry. Typical of the small family farm, the farmer kept a few of every kind of farm animal that could provide the necessary sources of food, and in some cases, a means to trade for other essential goods.

There were the two plow horses, Mike and Pat, three milk cows, a half-dozen goats, eight pigs and—as no farm would be complete without—as many chickens as you could collect.

Chickens were the absolute staple for every farm family in the 30's. They provided nearly everything you would need at minimal cost, and they required very little maintenance. Eggs were served in some form at virtually every meal. If you didn't eat the eggs, they were left under the hens to increase the flock by hatching a whole new generation of chicks. The chicken coop was well protected from any kind of predator and daily contact with the hens became somewhat of a social gathering.

Chickens are interesting characters. When they meander throughout a yard, they make a sound that really does resemble people speaking with each other. They are quite amusing, and our farmer friend found it to be as such. He became rather attached to his chickens and even began to befriend certain ones in a special and somewhat sentimental manner. Each time he would go out to feed his flock, there was one hen that would come close and seemingly communicate her affection for the farmer, recognizing him to be her source of provision. The farmer named this curious creature "Gerty," and he would look forward to being greeted by Gerty when delivering her meal. Gerty would come close to the farmer, eating the seed from his hand, and following him around the yard as he tended to the rest of the flock. The farmer and his chicken became personal friends in a way that was unique to only him and her. That relationship changed overnight, however, when the farmer left Gerty to hatch her eggs and produce her own family of chicks.

As usual, the farmer was out of bed early and out the door to begin his daily chores. He had not thought anything different of his daily tour around the farm, routinely hoisting hay for the cows, stopping to talk and comb Mike and Pat, throw some slop to the pigs, and chase a goat off the tractor seat for the umpteenth time. He strolled leisurely to the chicken coop, opening the door to release the hens into the yard for their daily walk and feast. To his utter surprise, however, when he opened the door to the hen house, a flurry of feathers and an ear-piercing screech attacked him from out of nowhere. It sent him striding backward, almost knocking him off of his feet. He was even more surprised when he realized that the assailant was none other than his good friend Gerty. The farmer collected himself and chuckled, realizing that Gerty was now the proud and protective mom of a family of seven tiny golden chicks. She was instinctively protecting her family—even from the farmer. For several days, Gerty made sure that nothing and no one was going to encroach within a safe distance of her family. The part of the story I remember so vividly from my childhood is what happened next.

Typical of a hot July day on the prairies, the farmer noticed on the horizon what he initially assumed was dust. To his horror, he realized that what he saw wasn't dust, but was, in fact, the smoke of a prairie fire moving swiftly toward his own farm. A fire in those days would spread several miles an hour, and this one was closing in rapidly.

In a panic, the farmer called his family out of the house and began to prepare for the inevitable. He had to protect his home and do his best to protect his critters. The fire engulfed his barn, his feed, and most of the surrounding trees, but he did manage to save his house by throwing water on it from the well and digging somewhat of a mote around his home.

Devastated and discouraged but not defeated after the fire passed, the farmer began to take stock of his losses. The ground was scorched with piles of debris and the charred remains of small structures. All he could do was wander somewhat aimlessly from object to object, remembering what was, and assessing the cost and work of replacing the essentials. The fire had left little in its path of that which could be salvaged. Feeling empty and stunned, our farmer friend walked by a lump of smoldering ash that looked every bit like the rest of the burnt remains in the yard. He wearily kicked the pile, and to his complete amazement and eventually to his delight, out from under the pile scurried seven little golden chicks.

Despite the devastation of the fire, life had been preserved in the form of a new generation of little chickens. A glimmer of hope began to well up within his heart. As he mused about the potential of rebuilding, it suddenly occurred to him, the pile of burnt rubble was, in fact, what remained of his good friend Gerty. The seven chicks were her family. She had literally given her life for her chicks. In the midst of overwhelming chaos, Gerty had gathered her little ones to herself, covering them with her own body and wings that they might be safe from the fatal flames of a powerful prairie fire. From her sacrifice and the surrender of her own life, a new generation would emerge, live, and flourish.

As I said, the story of Gerty left an indelible image in my mind of what it means to give cover to those you love and for whom you are responsible. Personal sacrifice, when not tarnished by sin, is in the DNA of all of creation. It is the intrinsic nature of creation to care for their young. It is the representation of a loving, caring, merciful God that has demonstrated the same ultimate sacrifice in the person of our Savior, Jesus.

True Biblical Headship

Our story gives us a great metaphor of what the principle of headship is all about. I love Philippians 2:6-8, because it portrays for us the truth of what it means to surrender our own lives for the lives and the care of those over whom we have been appointed. There is no room for selfishness. There is no room for personal ambition or manipulation at the expense of others.

True biblical headship is constantly under attack

Jesus "… emptied Himself, taking the form of a bond-servant …" (Philippians 2:7 NAS)

This surrender was not about self-promotion or self-preservation, it was about covering and stewardship.

True biblical headship is constantly under attack. The distortion of this principle, because of sin, is evidenced everywhere. Family breakdowns and men behaving like egotistical, controlling fools with their spouses and families are two clear indicators that we live in a society that has lost its way when it comes to embracing the true meaning and intent of family headship.

When godly headship is functioning properly, there is peace, harmony, and security. God does not leave that which He establishes to itself without structure. He designed the family to operate in a structured and orderly manner. When we do things His way, we see the wisdom and fruit of that design unfold as He intended.

Unfortunately, the Word of God is no longer society's guidebook for life. This has resulted in confusion and anger instead of joy and life.

Adam and Eve

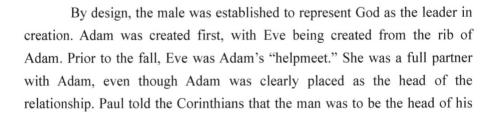

By design, the male was established to represent God as the leader in creation. Adam was created first, with Eve being created from the rib of Adam. Prior to the fall, Eve was Adam's "helpmeet." She was a full partner with Adam, even though Adam was clearly placed as the head of the relationship. Paul told the Corinthians that the man was to be the head of his wife and that Christ is the Head of man (1 Corinthians 11:13). If you understand the term "head" in the context of *covering* as opposed to *authority*, it becomes very liberating for everyone involved. Under a godly covering, we are free to grow and become everything God wants us to be, with a full sense of safety and security.

Adam and Eve's disobedience broke the purity of this union, bringing upon the future of mankind a curse that would impact and establish the foundation of Satan's assault against the family ever since. "To the woman he said, "I will make your pains in childbearing very severe; with painful labour you will give birth to children. **Your desire will be for your husband, and he will rule over you**" (Genesis 3:16). The statement *"your desire will be for your husband"* quite literally means that in an unredeemed state, the woman would long to control her husband, desiring to assume his place of headship. The flip side of that curse was that her husband would "rule over her." Built into the curse was the perfect storm of conflict; the woman longing for control and the man having the challenge of knowing and understanding the concept of ruler. Outside of a relationship submitted to Christ, this battle for control continues to rage on.

Our culture clearly reflects this struggle. God never intended for this relationship to be an authoritarian order. Mankind was structured in a way that mutual respect and submission to one another would allow for harmony and love. A man's role is to give leadership and to represent God to his family, not to dominate and overlord it …

> The youngest generation is being robbed of God's best

Now men, let me be clear. You have been given the position of "head" over your family tree. You are the patriarch. Your position has come under relentless assault, but if you abdicate your responsibility, you are not walking in accordance with God's divine intention for your family.

The family will see an immediate resurgence of life and restored health if men will take their place as the heads of their homes. The youngest generation is being robbed of God's best and is extremely vulnerable to spiritual attack when the grandfathers and fathers do not serve them as the physical, social, and spiritual heads in their homes. **Men of God, let's not allow that to happen on our watch.**

What has gone wrong? In the simplest terms, *covering* and *stewardship* have too often been replaced with *authority, domination, abuse,* and *manipulation.*

The life of Jesus doesn't reflect egotism and control, yet no one would ever question His headship and leadership in humanity. Jesus' ministry and life demonstrate the nurture, love, and care necessary for the healing and redemption of everyone He met. He wasn't confused about His role, nor was He insecure about serving those He was over. He didn't need to prove how important He was, nor did He feel inadequate when questioned. Jesus clearly understood and embraced His Father's mandate here on Earth. He is obviously the ultimate example of what true headship is meant to be.

Covering and Stewardship

The terms *covering* and *stewardship* best define what the role of the "head" or patriarch should be.

Covering

What is covering? The idea of covering suggests protective care. As the head of our home, men, it is our job to provide safety and security for our family. This refers not just to physical safety, but to an environment where all our family members can flourish and grow in all aspects of their lives. It is our job to nurture the home environment, leading it to be a place where family members can discover their personal identity and be proud of who God has made them to be. **"... love your wives, as Christ loved the church and gave himself up for her ..."** (Ephesians 5:25 ESV).

covering suggests protective care

Covering further implies that we must stand in the path of anything that might come against any members of the family. Moses declared in Deuteronomy 6:4-9 that it is our place to represent God to our family and to lead them into their own personal knowledge and experience with Him.

"Hear, O Israel: The LORD our God, the LORD is one. Love the LORD your God with all your heart and with all your soul and with all your strength. These commandments that I give you today are to be on your hearts. Impress them on your children. Talk about them when you sit at home and when you walk along the road, when you lie down and when you get up. Tie them as symbols on your hands and bind them on your foreheads. Write them on the door frames of your houses and on your gates."

It is our job to teach and lead our families, establishing Christ as Lord. Joshua's declaration **"... as for me and my household, we will serve the Lord ..."** is to be the mantra of the godly patriarch over his own home (Joshua 24:15).

We are like a spiritual umbrella on behalf of those God has given to our charge. We don't own or control anyone. We do, however, need to care, love, support, and nurture each one in such a way that they will know Jesus themselves.

Stewardship

What is stewardship? The dictionary defines stewardship as, "... a person who acts as the surrogate of another or others, ... the responsible overseeing and protection of something considered worth caring for and preserving ..."[7] The idea of stewardship suggests accountability. Every human being belongs to God.

> Each human being is ... fearfully and wonderfully made ...

The Bible says we are not our own but our bodies are the temple of the Holy Spirit (1 Corinthians 6:19). Every individual has their own direct and personal relationship with God. He loves each one as an individual. It is, however, God's design to create an infrastructure called *the family* to care for and nurture each person into a properly functioning vessel of God's glory. God has made each person and each family unique. Everyone is different; everyone is special. Each human being is **"...fearfully and wonderfully made..."** (Psalm 139:14). That is the beauty of creation.

As patriarchs, we are stewards of the lives of the children and grandchildren that are placed in our care and in our family tree. We will be required to give an answer for how we represent God to our family. The principle of headship places the responsibility on grandfathers and fathers to

---

[7] Stewardship. *In dictionary.com Online.* Retrieved from http://www.dictionary.com/browse/stewardship?s=t.

be accountable for each of these very special created beings. Our mission as the leaders and the heads of our families is to understand those uniquenesses and foster growth in each one in such a way that they might be able to reach the potential God has hardwired into them.

That is true leadership. That is godly headship. That is the way the system functions in harmony with God's divine order.

What Does Jacob Teach Us About Headship?

Our study of Genesis 48 and the patriarchal role Jacob had with Joseph and his family teach us a great deal about how we too, should serve in our own personal roles. Most cultures outside the Western world hold the elders of their families in far higher regard than we do in the West. Our secularized society has been, for years, diminishing the respect and honor of the head of our homes. Western culture is always looking for ways to remove the influence of the patriarch, while others are looking to draw from them.

I love the scene we are able to look in on from Genesis 48. Jacob clearly understood the responsibility he had as the family patriarch in the life of Joseph and his children.

A dear friend of mine made an insightful and astute observation that I had missed when writing this chapter. The anointing and the spiritual mantle on Jacob changed when Joseph showed up at his dad's house with his boys. The Scripture says in Genesis 48:2 that "Israel" got up off his bed to meet his son. He is not referred to as Jacob but rather as "Israel." Why is that important? We need to go back to Genesis 32:26-30 to understand the significance of this name change.

"Then the man said, "Let me go, for it is daybreak." But Jacob replied, "I will not let you go unless you bless me." The man asked him, "What is your name?" "Jacob," he answered. Then the man said, **"Your name will no longer be Jacob, but Israel, because you have struggled with God** and with humans and have overcome." Jacob said, "Please tell me your name." But he replied, "Why do you ask my name?" Then he blessed him there. So, Jacob called the place Peniel, saying, **"It is because I saw God face to face,** and yet my life was spared.""

Jacob was known as the "Deceiver" prior to this encounter with God. It was during that struggle that Jacob's life changed and that he could, from that night forward, be known as the man *who had struggled with God.* His experience that night changed his life forever. His personal understanding and perception of God would never be the same. He would never be the same.

Jacob didn't just know ABOUT God, he KNEW God, himself

Now, when he sat up to bless Joseph and his boys, he was doing it as the man who *had met God face to face.* No more theories, no more assumptions, no more philosophical assertions. Jacob had met God, struggled with God, and emerged a new man.

Men of God, this should be our greatest desire and contribution to the next generation. As we get older, we can reflect on the many times and experiences where we could fall into the category of *deceiver,* but let it be our story that we have met God *face to face* when passing blessing on to the next generations, that out of our personal struggles with God, we can speak genuinely and intimately of His faithfulness and love for all those who come before Him.

1 – Jacob's Position as Family Patriarch Was Highly Respected

"Some time later Joseph was told, "Your father is ill." **So he took his two sons** Manasseh and Ephraim along with him. When Jacob was told, "Your son Joseph has come to you," **Israel rallied his strength and sat up on the bed** (Genesis 48:1-2).

In this Scripture it is apparent that Joseph realized the need for his children to receive his father's patriarchal blessing. It is possible he had neglected this in his children's younger days, or maybe they weren't of age yet. Regardless, the passing on of blessing was something that Jacob must have instilled in Joseph from his childhood.

"… Then Joseph removed them from Israel's knees and bowed down with his face to the ground …" (Genesis 48:12). Joseph heard his dad was dying, so he hastily made his way to his dad's bedside. The Scriptures say that as soon as Jacob heard Joseph had arrived, he rallied his strength, got up off the couch and immediately began to discuss the blessing of God with his son. Joseph's posture, his humility, and his honor for his father tell you all you need to know about the degree of respect he had for his dad.

There was obviously an intense appreciation for the role of the patriarch. Joseph was a powerful man and in the natural, certainly didn't need his dad to provide him with anything. I believe what Joseph did understand was that something would be missing in the form of spiritual covering embodied by his dad, and he didn't want to miss that for either himself or his family.

It is something that we as the heads of our own families should discuss, teach, and communicate to our own sons and daughters. There can be a lot of misunderstanding in family relationships today that can prevent members of the family from receiving what God has for them. As the patriarch, we should find ways and means to educate our families about the power of blessing, and help them to appreciate the role of the patriarch as a steward of that which is ultimately God's.

2 – Jacob Understood the Value, Power, and Order of Blessing

a) **JACOB UNDERSTOOD THE VALUE, POWER, AND ORDER OF BLESSING**

"Jacob said to Joseph, "God Almighty appeared to me at Luz in the land of Canaan, **and there he blessed me** and said to me …" (Genesis 48:3).

Jacob's life had been anything but a straight line. In fact, as previously noted, his name literally meant "Deceiver." There were lots of ups and downs, and he had a long history of narrow scrapes. The one thing that had sustained him in his

Jacob had heard the voice of God

life, however, was his knowledge that at *Luz,* God had blessed him. He knew what it meant to cling to the hope that comes with the blessing of God. He knew first-hand what God had given him, and he wanted each of his children and their children to know that same blessing.

When you own something precious, something that might be irreplaceable, you treasure and protect it because you know its value. Jacob understood the value of blessing.

When Joseph brought his boys to be prayed for, Jacob knew that this was an incredibly valuable responsibility he was about to exercise.

b) JACOB HAD WITNESSED THE POWER OF GOD FOR HIMSELF

"… **I am going to make you** fruitful and increase your numbers. **I will make you** a community of peoples, **and I will give** this land as an everlasting possession to your descendants after you' …." (Genesis 48:4).

Jacob had heard the voice of God. When you hear God, there is nothing that compares to it. The power and strength that comes through His voice leads you through your whole life. Vision, passion, energy, and determination accompany His voice. A man convinced of the calling of God cannot be deterred from his mission. As the "head" of his family, Jacob knew that God had promised him something that must, in turn, be conferred upon his sons and their families. Jacob knew that the voice and promises of God were for all the generations in his family tree. He knew that God was powerful and eager for his descendants to hear His voice the same way he had.

When God speaks in first person to someone as He did to Jacob, they listen. Jacob had witnessed the power of God himself and knew how real that power was.

As he prepared to pray over his grandsons, Jacob knew what a powerful spiritual impartation and journey he was about to commission into the lives of these boys.

c) HE UNDERSTOOD THERE WAS A DIVINE ORDER CONNECTING THE GENERATIONS

"Then **he blessed Joseph** and said, "May the God before whom **my fathers Abraham and Isaac** walked faithfully, the God who has **been my shepherd all my life** to this day, the Angel who has delivered me from all harm—**may he bless these boys. May they** be called by my name and the names of my fathers Abraham and Isaac, and may they increase greatly on the earth" (Genesis 48:15-16).

Jacob understood headship and the role his forefathers played in his own journey and the role they were going to play in the journey of Joseph and his sons. Jacob names five generations in his prayer. He establishes that his **"father Abraham and his father Isaac" were blessed and called by God, and then declares that God, who had led him as a "shepherd his whole life," should now bless the fourth generation, Joseph, and the fifth-generation, Ephraim and Manasseh, the same way.**

Order of Headship in Genesis 48

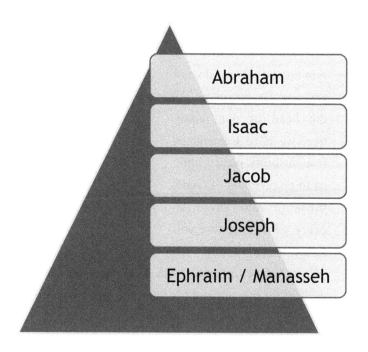

The headship principle is defined through the naming of these five generations. Abraham was not alive when Jacob lived, but there is clearly a connection that God sees as important enough to include it in the Scriptures.

Jacob understood that he was one more link in the patriarchal cord enhancing God's connection with Ephraim and Manasseh. He embraced the responsibility of "headship" in his family as a means of passing God's favor on to them. It wasn't just a "be a nice grandpa" thing, it was, in fact, a spiritual imperative.

3 – Jacob Had Something to Give

Fulfilling the place of the patriarch and serving in a godly headship role requires us to pay attention to our own lives and our own personal walk with God. If we are stewards of those placed in our care, then what we have to give them is a serious matter.

We must be constantly reminded that we do not just live for ourselves. As the head of our family tree, we have tremendous responsibility placed upon us to be conduits of God's blessing and favor to every generation that will follow us.

> We must be constantly reminded that we do not just live for ourselves

Jacob's experience with God was the very thing Joseph desired for himself and his family and the very thing Jacob could pass on.

a) GOD APPEARED TO JACOB

"Jacob said to Joseph, "**God Almighty appeared to me** at Luz in the land of Canaan ..." (Genesis 48:3).

Having our own personal experience and story of an encounter with God enables us to speak with conviction and strength. Jacob didn't just know about God. He KNEW God himself. He could tell the story of how the Lord met him and spoke with him. He could tell of life-altering experiences and the personal joy of having met the Lord in a special and significant way.

As the heads of our homes and families, it is critical that we be constantly developing our personal walk with Jesus. It is our personal relationship and experience with Christ that makes the passing on of blessing such a powerful influence.

b)   THERE GOD BLESSED HIM

"…and there **he blessed me** and said to me …" (Genesis 48:3).

We established in an earlier chapter that the word "bless" literally means "To invoke God for the purpose of prospering." Jacob knew first-hand how God made things happen in ways that only He could. He had seen the prosperity that came from God's blessing. He had the joy of being reunited with his own son when for years, he had presumed him dead. As the head of his family, Jacob could pass on the very hope and assurance that comes from witnessing God's favor in a personal and powerful way.

The Apostle Paul instructed the Thessalonians to **"… give thanks in everything for this is the will of God" (1 Thessalonians 5:13)**. I recall as a kid an old hymn that was sung in church on a regular basis.

Count your blessings, name them one by one, count your many blessings and see what God has done.

Too often we lose sight of God's blessings in our lives. It is these blessings, however, when recounted, which serve as a tremendous testimony of His goodness to us and a reminder of the hope we have in Christ.

God's blessing is our story. Recount those blessings and tell your story to your own grandchildren and children.

c) GOD GAVE HIM PROMISES

'I am going to make you fruitful and will increase your numbers. I will make you a community of peoples, and I will give this land as an everlasting possession to your descendants after you' (Genesis 48:4).

The promises of God change a person's life. As the head of our families, the greatest thing we can pass on is a knowledge of the Word of God and His promises to us as believers. When His promises are real to us, then we can make them real to our grandchildren and children. *"I have stored up your word in my heart ... "* (Psalm 119:11 ESV).

Jacob reiterated the promises God had made to him, knowing full well those promises went beyond him and were very much for Joseph and his family as well.

What has the Lord said to you? Which of His promises are the most precious and meaningful to you? As the head of your family, you become the voice of those promises for the next generation. You have the privilege of shaping the journey of that generation by passing on those promises, making them real, powerful, and personal to your own descendants.

Jacob understood he was the patriarch, the "head" of his family. He knew that what he had to give would shape the very destiny of his grandchildren.

The Significant Role of Grandfathers

Grampa, you are the head of your family tree. You have been commissioned with the charge of providing spiritual cover for your family; to be a steward of those whom the Lord has placed in your care. Represent God well and pass on His blessing. Set the course for their lives. Recognize the privilege and responsibility you have to be a part of the next great move of God by fulfilling your headship role faithfully as unto the Lord.

THE WRESTLING MATCH

Chapter 6

"Spiritual warfare is very real. There is a furious, fierce, and ferocious battle raging in the realm of the spirit between the forces of God and the forces of evil. Warfare happens every day, all the time. Whether you believe it or not, you are in a battlefield. You are in warfare."

Pedro Okoro

THIS IS A REAL RING-A-DING-DONG-DANDY. THE FAMILIAR CATCHPHRASE OF the legendary Ed Whalen, with his very distinguishable voice, would sound out across the TV airwaves every Saturday afternoon. It was undeniable pronouncement of another "Battle Royale" of Stampede Wrestling. Before Mr. Whalen would bid the audience farewell or declare, "In the meantime and in-between time, this is another edition of Stampede Wrestling," the likes of Abdullah the Butcher, Gene Kiniski, and André the Giant would have rolled around the mats and jumped off the top ropes of the wrestling ring. Gorgeous George, Stu Hart, and the Cuban Assassin would have bludgeoned one another with foreign objects, and Tor Kamata would have thrown salt into the eyes of Archie "the Stomper" Gouldie, followed by a nasty judo chop to the throat, rendering him immobile, and regaining the prized championship belt. This was entertainment in its rawest form.

I remember those days vividly; so captivating and shrouded in mystery. Were these matches even real? Did the opponents travel together from venue to venue in the same station wagon, dining together in the same restaurants and sharing hotel rooms? Or were they really the arch enemies of one another as portrayed on TV?

Only Ed Whalen, Stu Hart, and the combatants themselves knew for sure. Well, pretty much everyone else knew also, but nobody wanted to come out and say it. After all, there was no better theatre for the male audience in the 60's, 70's, and 80's.

Good verses evil. The enticement and energy of such battles continue to be waged in the arena of life at every level. The concept of such warfare typifies the ongoing challenges that we as believers, and specifically Christian men, are faced with each and every day of our lives as we seek to understand and follow the leading of the "Captain of Hosts," our Lord Jesus.

The Bible frequently depicts the spiritual war that takes place in the realm of the unseen. It is a battle for the lives, minds, and souls of all of mankind; a battle that rages and is fought in such a way that if we are not aware of the tactics and strategies employed, we can become victims of a foe that is determined to kill, steal, and destroy.

The Battle is Real–Understanding That is the First Step to Walking in Victory

Behind the veil of everyday life, lurking in the shadows, cloaked in mystery and confusion, is our spiritual enemy. Satan is real. Angels, demons, spiritual warfare—they all exist whether you believe it or not.

*"Be alert and of sober mind. **Your enemy the devil prowls around like a roaring lion** looking for someone to devour. Resist him, standing firm in the faith ... "*(1 Peter 5:8-9).

Satan is real. Angels, demons, spiritual warfare— they all exist

*"For though we live in the world, we do not wage war as the world does. The weapons we fight with are not the weapons of the world. On the contrary, they have **divine power to demolish strongholds**"* (2 Corinthians 10:3-4).

*"For in him all things were created, things in heaven and on earth, **visible and invisible**, whether **thrones or powers or rulers or authorities;** all things have been created through him and for him"* (Colossians 1:16).

In Ephesians 6:12, the apostle Paul presents a divine revelation he received that describes how Satan's kingdom has been militarily aligned. He writes, *"For we do not wrestle against flesh and blood, but against principalities, against powers, against the rulers of the darkness of this age, against spiritual hosts of wickedness in heavenly places"* (NKJV).

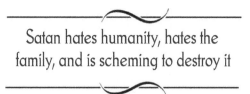

Satan hates humanity, hates the family, and is scheming to destroy it

The Greek word for *wrestle* here means "man to man combat to the death."[8] It was used to describe two Greek wrestlers who fought to the death. As believers, we are involved in a spiritual battle with Satan and the kingdom of darkness, where he is determined to eradicate mankind. Satan hates humanity, hates the family, and is scheming to destroy it.

It is important to understand the way Satan sets up his dark forces because it will help us to understand why the attack on the patriarchs is such a tactical move of the devil and his spiritual military. The organization of this kingdom is clearly outlined in Ephesians 6:12 (KJV):

... against the principalities, against the powers, against the rulers of the darkness of this age, and against spiritual hosts of wickedness in the heavenly places ..."

There are at least five different levels of authority within the satanic kingdom. At the top is Satan or Lucifer, who is in command. However, below him are four different ranks of his assigned henchmen.

The following categories help us to see how structured and organized his kingdom is:[9]

1. **PRINCIPALITIES** (*Archas*) - highest ranking beings

2. **POWERS** (*Exousias*) - powers of authority

3. **RULERS** (*Kosmokratoras*) - world rulers of the spiritual darkness

4. **SPIRITUAL HOSTS OF WICKEDNESS** (*Ponerias*) - wicked spirits

---

[8] Wooldridge, K. *The 24 Doctrines of the Bible Spiritual Warfare.* Retrieved from http://www.kenwooldridge.org/OBC-DOCT-17.HTML

[9] Wooldridge, K. *The 24 Doctrines of the Bible Spiritual Warfare.* Retrieved from http://www.kenwooldridge.org/OBC-DOCT-17.HTML

Rick Renner of Rick Renner Ministries[10] has done extensive studies on the subject of spiritual warfare and I have gleaned a great deal from his writings. I have paraphrased some of Mr. Renner's conclusions and how he has described the rank and file of Satan's forces in the following paragraphs.

Notice that at the top of this list, Paul mentions a group of evil spirits he calls **PRINCIPALITIES.** It is used to depict individuals who hold the highest position of rank and authority. Paul tells us that they are the top of Satan's kingdom and are powerful evil beings that have held their lofty positions of power and authority since ancient times—probably ever since the fall of Lucifer.

Paul goes on to tell us that the evil forces, second in command in Satan's dark kingdom, are a group of principalities he refers to as **POWERS.** These are demon spirits who have received delegated authority from Satan to carry out all manner of evil in whatever way they can.

The third level Paul mentions is **RULERS OF THIS DARK WORLD.** This phrase described military training camps where young men were assembled, trained, and turned into a mighty army. This level of recruits were the special forces. They were just raw power when they first arrived in the training camp, however, as their training progressed and the young men were taught discipline and order, all that raw aggression was converted into an organized, disciplined army.

This methodical approach tells you and me that Satan is so serious about doing damage to the human race that he deals with demon spirits as though they are troops! He puts them in rank and file, gives them orders and assignments, and then sends them out like military soldiers who are committed

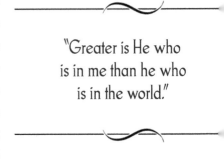

"Greater is He who is in me than he who is in the world."

[10]https://renner.org/renner-tv/what-the-bible-says-about-spiritual-warfare-part-2/

to killing. Just as men in a human army are equipped and trained in their methods of destruction, so, too, are these demon spirits. And once these demons are trained and ready to start their assault, Satan sends them forth to do their devious work against human beings.

The Apostle Paul names a fourth level of rank he calls **SPIRITUAL WICKEDNESS.** These are the "Privates" but are still vile, evil, and wicked in every way. They thirst for power and wreak havoc any way they can.

There is no doubt that Satan has a plan to destroy humanity and the family by any means necessary. The exciting and reassuring truth, though, is that greater is He who is in me than he who is in the world (1 John 4:4). Jesus promised "… I have overcome the world …" (John 16:33). Paul defines this victory succinctly in Colossians 2:15 (ESV), **He disarmed the rulers and authorities and put them to open shame, by triumphing over them in him.**

A Closer Look at Ephesians 6:10-12

10 Finally, my brethren, be strong in the Lord and in the power of His might. 11 Put on the whole armor of God, that you may be able to stand against the wiles of the devil. 12 For we do not wrestle against flesh and blood, but against principalities, against powers, against the rulers of the darkness of this age, against spiritual hosts of wickedness in the heavenly places. 13 Therefore take up the whole armor of God, that you may be able to withstand in the evil day, and having done all, to stand. 14 Stand therefore … Ephesians 6:10—14 NKJV

There are six truths identified in these verses that define the spiritual wrestling match of which we, as the patriarchs in our families, must be mindful. These truths will help us to better approach our role as men of God and the heads of our family tree.

1) **Verse 11—THE FIGHT IS STRATEGIC AND INTENTIONAL.** The word for *wiles*, or another translation calls it *schemes*, literally means a "diabolical plot." Satan has a scheme happening. It is a diabolical ploy to destroy God's ultimate creation—us—the family.

   Satan and his minions are working 24/7 on a strategy to break down and destroy humanity. This is important to understand because when you look at what has obviously been a slow melting of Christian values, principles, and truths in society, it becomes clear that this assault has been by design. As any military leader, Satan surrounds himself with his forces to scheme up and employ tactics that are intended to dissolve God's order.

   There are no such things as random events in history. There is a spiritual chess match that is always being orchestrated. Satan is patient and deliberate in his maneuvers. Even though we know he is defeated, he will not quit until the final judgment.

   Our families are his target. When you analyze the attacks that have come against the home, it is very apparent that families have indeed, been the focus of these assaults. Thankfully, we have the promise and the hope of victory through Jesus. However, being ignorant of Satan's intentions is extremely unwise.

2) **Verse 12—THIS WRESTLING MATCH IS NOT AGAINST PEOPLE.** I must admit, it can be frustrating and very difficult to remember this point. When I listen to people campaign for things that I know to be clear violations of biblical truth, I can get quite emotional about it and

angry at the person. It is, however, contrary to the Word of God to do that.

Paul was clear. Our fight is not against other people. We established in an earlier chapter that human beings carry the DNA of God, and that how we treat them is action directed toward their Creator. As difficult as it may be

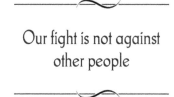

Our fight is not against other people

sometimes, we must direct our energy against the spiritual forces that are behind the evil that we see unfolding in many areas of present-day life. Even though the people may be motivated by wicked ambition and behave in ungodly and unrighteous ways, we still must remember, Jesus died for them as well. Satan is using them like puppets to carry out his diabolical scheme. They don't even realize it.

I believe it is imperative for us, as men of God, to stand up and defend truth and defend our families, but in doing so we must remember that the fight is still waged against spiritual forces that are using human agents to carry out the scheme. We begin the defense of our homes by praying against the forces that are behind the people carrying out enemy plans.

3) **Verse 12—THE FIGHT IS AGAINST SPIRITUAL FORCES.** As already been established, there is an unseen spiritual enemy we are continually opposing. The Scriptures articulate the battleground as being one that is resident in the unseen. War against the enemy has been won in the Spirit through the work of Jesus, and the ground must be secured in the spirit through the righteousness of Christ, His shed blood, and the power of His Word established in faith.

4) **Verse 12—THERE IS A HIERARCHY OF FORCES TO CONTEND WITH.** We have defined the hierarchy of forces that

work against us, but it is important at this point to explain the significance of that relative to us as the patriarchs in our families. The question needs to be asked, **"Why is Satan so focused on attacking the role of men in our society, and more specifically, their role in the home?"**

As in any military system and combat scenario, the ultimate quest is to topple the leadership of your enemy. If you can separate the troops from their leader, you leave that platoon weak and vulnerable. Satan understands and recognizes the way God designed the family. The patriarch, the grandfathers, and the fathers are the heads of

You are God's assigned agent to provide covering and care to your home

their families. It is their job to care for, lead, and protect their homes. If Satan can remove that leader from the battle, the rest of the family members are far more susceptible to attack. The social and spiritual order of humanity is structured in the same way Satan's armies are organized. God established men as the leaders of the human race. When that system can be broken down, mankind becomes an easy target.

The assault on this orderly structure has come in the form of displacing the fathers as heads of their homes. Even more specifically, it begins by having the patriarchs of the families—the grandfathers:

1) become increasingly more disengaged or
2) having them administer dominant control and manipulation, leaving the family living in fear or alienation.

Without patriarchs properly functioning as the godly headship, the family unit becomes extremely vulnerable to the enemy's ploys. Just as the body cannot function the way it was designed when there is a problem with the head, neither can the family live in a healthy way with one another without being under the proper headship covering of the family patriarch. A healthy head makes for a healthy body.

Grampa … Dad … Can you begin to see how valuable you are and how important it is for you to be totally engaged in the lives and leadership of your family? You are God's assigned agent to provide covering and care to your home.

5) **Verse 12—THEY ARE OVER THIS PRESENT DARKNESS.**
This present darkness. What does that mean? The world is in an unclaimed state. Even though Jesus has provided redemption for mankind, the earth and those who have not accepted Christ's atonement remain under the control of the spiritual forces to which Adam forfeited them. Paul calls it "this present darkness." The sin and wickedness that shroud our current state is a strong indication that Satan is indeed, the "god of this world." Jesus teaches that even though we are in this world, we are not of this world. We live in this darkness, but we are, in fact, seated in heavenly places in Christ Jesus (Ephesians 2:6).

We are clothed in light. We are the righteousness of Christ, but we must continue the wrestling match in this dark world until all of creation experiences the full redemptive power of Jesus.

> We are the righteousness of Christ but we must continue the wrestling match

This present darkness is the world order, as can be witnessed in the natural, unrighteous, and unholy acts of a lost humanity. The direction of our society reflects the scheme that Satan has been working on for decades. The social issues that have been rapidly emerging as *normal* all have their root in the same fundamental strategy. So many of the challenges that currently affect our society have a common denominator—the removal, dismissal, and disengagement of men as leaders in our homes, communities, churches, and nations. The emergence of the present-day cry of "Times have changed" all have a basic baseline reality: the assault on men as the heads and patriarchs the way God designed it.

Look at the following social challenges:

➤ The "traditional family" change
➤ Divorce
➤ Sexual identity confusion
➤ Pornography
➤ Single parent homes
➤ Abortion
➤Youth Crime
➤ Promiscuous lifestyles, adulterous living
➤ Extreme feminism
➤ Secularism in education
➤ Unfiltered sin in entertainment
➤ Disengaged fatherhood in family relationships

Each of these issues can be a flashpoint in our current secular and liberal culture, and regardless of whether or not everyone agrees on the significance of them, I can say without reservation that each issue has largely emerged because of the absence of godly male leadership. When a godly, dependent-on-Christ man steps up and gives oversight, covering, protection, and leadership, these issues begin to lose their strength.

A man committed to the Word of God and who has a heart surrendered to Jesus will bring light into this present darkness. When we do things God's way, light dispels darkness and life rises out of death and defeat.

6) **Verse 12—THEY ARE EVIL.** I believe it needs to be stated clearly and emphatically, at this point, that there is nothing innocent or benign about the tactics of the enemy. The social challenges previously listed are not just a shift in opinions. They are the result of evil strategies intended for the annihilation, destruction, and elimination of humanity. We have been duped into believing we are just old fashioned, out-of-touch dinosaurs in a more "progressive and enlightened" society. We are told we live in the past and there is no way to stop the move toward a more liberal and tolerant culture. Let me declare as loudly as I know how. **THAT IS A LIE!** It is very much a part of the scheme. It is very much a part of the evil ploy, of this present darkness, led by Satan himself, with all of his forces that are working for him.

If we don't call it for what it is—evil—we will fall into the trap of believing that our role has been so diminished that we cannot make a difference and we cannot salvage the current generation of children and all that will follow them.

The Apostle Paul's plea to the Ephesians was clear and strong. Paul said after you have done everything, to stand, "Stand Firm" after you understand what is going on. Do not be deceived. It is time to take a strong stand. It was a call to arms. He meticulously describes the battle gear for the fight.

> Stand therefore, having girded your waist with truth, having put on the breastplate of righteousness, and having shod your feet with the preparation of the gospel of peace; above all, taking the shield of faith with which you will be able to quench all the fiery darts of the wicked one. And take the helmet of salvation, and the sword of the Spirit, which is the word of God; praying always with all prayer and supplication in the Spirit, being watchful to this end with all perseverance and supplication for all the saints ...
>
> Ephesians 6:14-18 (NKJV)

Ephesians chapter 6 is a vivid and detailed account of what the battle looks like, how the enemy works, and the beseeching of believers to take up the fight to destroy the enemy and his schemes. It is my deep conviction that the MEN of God play a primary and critical role in this fight. You are the generals—the head of your own personal brigade. If you engage, you can establish righteousness in your own camp and significantly contribute to what God is doing throughout the world.

Our Hope Is in Jesus

Below are several verses that, as a grandfather and family patriarch, we can commit to memory while taking our stand against the "schemes of the devil" on behalf of our families.

✦ 2 Corinthians 10:4—*For the weapons of our warfare are not of the flesh but have divine power to destroy strongholds.* (ESV)

✦ Colossians 2:15—*He disarmed the rulers and authorities and put them to open shame, by triumphing over them in him.* (ESV)

✦ James 4:7—*Submit yourselves therefore to God. Resist the devil, and he will flee from you.* (ESV)

✦ 1 John 4:4—*You are from God, little children, and have overcome them; because greater is He who is in you than he who is in the world.* (NKJV)

✦ 2 Corinthians 10:3-5—*For though we live in the world, we do not wage war as the world does. The weapons we fight with are not the weapons of the world. On the contrary, they have divine power to demolish strongholds. We demolish arguments and every pretension that sets itself up against the knowledge of God, and we take captive every thought to make it obedient to Christ.*

✦ Romans 8:37—*In all these things we are more than conquerors through Him who loved us.*

✦ 1 Corinthians 15:57—*But thanks be to God! He gives us the victory through our Lord Jesus Christ.*

To receive your **FREE** *Grampa's Time* Self-study booklet, just email cal@grampastime.com and request a copy. I will gladly send you one if it will assist you in your journey of becoming the patriarch God has called you to be.

For speaking engagements, workshop presentations, or conferences, please contact Cal at calellerby@nucleus.com.

Watch for the upcoming small group study resource and other books designed to encourage and enhance your walk with Christ as the head of your home, your church, and your community.

The "Grampa's Time" ministry exists to:
"Enlist, Equip, Encourage, and Empower 1,000,000 Grandfathers and Fathers to Lay hands on their Grandchildren and Children, Speaking the Blessing of God into their Lives."

Section Two

THE IMPARTATION

Embrace Your Patriarchal Appointment

Chapter 7   STEP 1

I HAD JUST FINISHED A GRAMPA'S TIME PRESENTATION FOR A GROUP OF ABOUT thirty guys and was in the process of packing up my things getting ready to head home, when I was approached by an obviously emotional gentleman. I will call him John, as in John Doe. He was about sixty years old, well dressed and looking very much like many of the men who have attended my workshops or presentations. He was a bit standoffish, apparently not wanting to interrupt my activities, and yet definitely eager to express something that had clearly impacted him. His eyes were red and it seemed obvious that he had been significantly moved during the presentation.

I stopped what I was doing and extended my hand, introducing myself. He did likewise, but as soon as he said his name the tears began to well up in his eyes, albeit he was doing his best, like all proud guys, to control any indication of weakness, choking back the emotion that was literally on the verge of public display. In a somewhat broken and humble voice, he said to me, "I want to thank you."

Assuming he had enjoyed and identified with the presentation and challenge, I responded with a rhetorical, "You're welcome. I appreciate the encouragement." John's facial expression told me there was more to his gratitude than merely a general gesture of appreciation. He had experienced something that was deeper than I had initially assumed. The emotion he was displaying reflected a discovery he had encountered during the session that would open a whole new world for him as a man.

What Was it that had Connected so Deeply with my New Friend's Heart?

The comments John made have been repeated many times by other men who have attended our workshops. His thoughts are definitely on the forefront of many men's minds, having been subjected to decades of misleading and even intentional assaults on their manhood.

With genuine sincerity, John said **"Thank you for giving me a place. I didn't know where I fit or even that I belonged."** This statement has entrenched a conviction in me personally that has proven to be a strong indicator that God is doing something

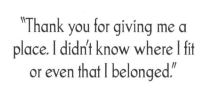

"Thank you for giving me a place. I didn't know where I fit or even that I belonged."

powerful in men around the world.

As our conversation continued, John began to define a relationship with his family that I have heard over and over again from men across the country; guys who have been successful in business, have had many milestones and achievements in life, but have felt detached and often ineffective in their role as a father and a grandfather. Like so many, John had fallen victim to the lie that his role had largely been fulfilled and that his place as an influencer was, for the most part, in the past. John was discouraged and felt impotent in his function as a dad and grampa.

The spiritual forces with which we wrestle have, for decades, been working through the channels of education, entertainment, politics and so on, to minimize and displace the influence and leadership of the patriarchs. It is Satan's plan to convince men they should be **"seen and not heard."** This ongoing lie is part of a diabolical scheme in the never-ending battle for the generations.

We are witnessing the fruit of a culture and society that has been largely void of godly headship. Mass confusion, chaos, and an almost completely dismantled family structure has resulted in broken hearts, fractured lives, and a world that is hopelessly trying to find its way without God. I am seeing men everywhere like John, looking for answers, longing to understand their role, and diligently seeking the Lord for a fresh experience with Jesus so the next generation can live under God's favor.

King David prayed with passion in Psalm 71:18

Now also when I am old and grayheaded, O God, do not forsake me, Until I declare Your strength to this generation, Your power to everyone who is to come. (NKJV)

Sharing with men from all kinds of backgrounds and listening to the stories of many, I have concluded that if we are going to see a national movement of patriarchal leaders, God is going to need to bring deep healing into the lives of guys. The emotional and spiritual brokenness of men runs deep.

I recall having sat with three older grandfathers following one of our workshops, each of whom had their own stories of pain they had carried throughout their whole lives. Taking turns, they spoke of how their childhoods were not great, and how they felt guilty for being what they considered to be poor fathers to their own children. They communicated to me, a man, how they wished God would allow them to have a "do-over" as a dad.

It was heart-wrenching to see these older gentlemen, who had been successful in the world's eyes, feel so wounded and disappointed with themselves.

As with these fellows, however, it is always very exciting to see God do great things in men of all stripes as we pray together in repentance for the healing of their souls. It's satisfying to hear guys stand up and say, **"Thank you for giving me a place."**

Men Need to be Healed

Having talked with men across the country and having sought the Lord for clarity on what the issues of their brokenness are, I have concluded there are approximately seven root causes keeping men from engaging as the patriarchs God has appointed them to be. Like any root system, there are many limbs associated with these struggles and I, in no way, can identify all of them. However, I do feel that unmasking the following seven tentacles is a realistic place to start when approaching God for the healing of grandfather's and father's hearts.

If we are going to mobilize the patriarchs as key players in the restoration of our families, communities, and nations, we must believe God can and will bring healing to their lives.

7 Roots of Disablement:

1) **HAVING BEEN POORLY FATHERED**—In the generation of grandfathers, this is a common challenge. For many older men especially, they have a common plight in that their fathers were basically absent as they grew up. Stories of harsh words and excessive discipline have left an entire segment of our world feeling inadequate and weak as men. Whatever the root of this detachment from their fathers, a large percentage of senior men have spent much of their lives looking for the acceptance and approval they never received from their dads.

2) **LIVING WITH REGRETS**—Being weighed down with disappointment and discouragement because of bad choices, poor modeling, or unacceptable behavior, is an emotionally crippling tactic of the enemy. Whether real or perceived, once the heaviness of these feelings takes root, it can become extremely difficult to become free to believe you can still play a significant role as a spiritual leader and influencer. The reality is this—some guys are guilty of some very wrong choices, while others wish they simply would have taken better approaches to being a dad or grampa. Regardless of where you are on the spectrum, it is necessary for

you to get free from guilt, shame, and disappointment, so God can use you the way He wants to.

3) **BELIEVING SOCIETY'S LIE**—Men have been indoctrinated for years that their role is not valued. Confusion about where they fit is common. Abdicating responsibility as a grandfather and father are expected because of the spiritual oppression against strong, godly leadership from men. Because much of our society has chosen to eliminate the Scriptures as a guiding roadmap in life, we have men going off the rails as leaders, giving justification to the notion that they are sexist, chauvinist, controlling, and overbearing people that can't be trusted. That is the message being projected on the earth; so much so that too many men, even Christian men, have lost their conviction and resolve to be godly leaders for fear of being seen as such.

4) **DEMANDS OF LIFE**—Stress is a deceitful and subversive ploy in Satan's arsenal of weapons. Money, time, resources, careers, relationships ... the list can go on and on. Life is busy and demanding and what we find most demanding always seems to take our time and attention—even if it's not necessarily what is the most important. We all experience the constant vacuum which has an insatiable appetite for our attention and affections. If we don't control these demands and bring them into submission to Christ, we will lose our ability to experience God's best for ourselves and those He has given to our covering and stewardship.

5) **SIN**—The secret world of men is usually what destroys them. All too often guys are controlled by issues that few people know about. Sin forces us into patterns that are not only destructive to our personal lives and those around us, but it also stymies any

hope of effective service in the Kingdom. Sin creates guilt and condemnation, it robs of vision and expectation, and imposes shame, disappointment, and discouragement. The devil uses sin cleverly to convince us there is no hope; that our failures are so insurmountable that God would never allow us to be free and forgiven. Thankfully, the Scriptures declare that *"...while we were still sinners, Christ died for us ... "* (Romans 5:8).

6) **LAZINESS**— *"A little sleep, a little slumber, a little folding of the hands to rest— and poverty will come on you like a thief and scarcity like an armed man"* (Proverbs 24:33-34). We don't always have the energy or the motivation to actively fulfill our mandate as the patriarch, but it can also be a spiritual tactic of the enemy to leave the next generation vulnerable. Jacob, while he was on his deathbed in Genesis 48, rallied his strength and rose up from his bed to bless Joseph and his boys.

7) **FEAR**—The fear of rejection, the fear of failure, the fear of man. It is so unfortunate that men who have been created with an intrinsic warrior heart can be defeated by fear. It is almost as if we don't know how to differentiate between fighting aggressively and still gently and courageously leading. I have witnessed too many men who shrink back from their role as a patriarch because they have concluded others to be more spiritual, more gifted, or smarter than themselves. They lose sight of the call of God on their lives, and in so doing, those around them who truly need them, are denied. Remember *"God has not given us a spirit of fear"* (2 Timothy 1:7 NLT).

How do we overcome these disablements? The Apostle James gives us some simple and clear instruction to receive healing in these areas.

Therefore, confess your sins to one another [your false steps, your offenses], and pray for one another, that you may be healed and restored. The heartfelt and persistent prayer of a righteous man (believer) can accomplish much [when put into action and made effective by God—it is dynamic and can have tremendous power].

James 5:16 (AMP)

The Healing Process

1) **Confess to one another**—Share your heart. Share your struggles. Share your story. Hold one another accountable. Find a friend or join a small group.

2) **Pray for one another**—Lay hands on one another, anoint each other with oil.

3) **Receive forgiveness**

4) **Embrace truth**—The Word of God declares us forgiven. Jesus assures us He has overcome the world. Hide His Word in your heart.

5) **Walk in newness of life**—Choose to walk in righteousness.

Our Ultimate Goal is to Get in the Game

Getting free from the debilitating vices waged against us is critically important. However, it can't stop there. There is a battle to be won; a war to be fought for the hearts and lives of a whole new generation. There is a new sound on the horizon—the sound of God's voice calling men of God from every corner of the nation to take their place in Kingdom service. Men of God, rise up and embrace your appointed role as the patriarchs in society and make yourselves available to the Kingdom as leaders and primary influencers in your families, in your churches, in your communities, and in our nations.

I like the imagery of "rising up." It makes me think of Jacob in Genesis 48:2. He heard his son Joseph was coming, and even though he was very ill, the Bible says, **"He rallied his strength and sat up on the bed."** Despite his sickness and his weakness, Jacob refused to lay down. I find that so inspirational. The challenge is too important, the stakes are too high. There is too much to lose for us as men of God, to not be engaged.

Jacob Understood What to Do

At the beginning of this chapter, I introduced you to John. When John experienced his personal epiphany about who he was and what his role was as the patriarch in his family, his comment to me, again, was, "Thank you for giving me a place." I have heard that statement, or variations of it, many times from men all over the country. There is a divine awakening happening amongst men that is setting them free from obscurity.

As often as I have heard that statement, there is a question that is asked along with it, which requires even more attention. The question is simply this: **"What do I do? I need help to know how to engage as the patriarch in my family."** My observation of men is that they prefer structure when being asked to serve in this capacity. Give them some order and a framework and the likelihood of them engaging goes way up.

Jacob has a lot to teach us in this area as well. I will give specific instruction on what to do next in the following chapters, but I would like to point out some significant observations from Jacob's experience that can help answer the question, **"What do we do as a family patriarch?"** Jacob's personal motivations are revealed and helpful for our own quest to embrace our appointment as the head of our families.

Genesis 48:8-11

*8 When Israel **saw the sons** of Joseph, he asked, **"Who are these?"** 9 "They are the sons God has given me here," Joseph said to his father. Then Israel said, **"Bring them to me so I may bless them."** 10 Now Israel's eyes were failing because of old age, and he could hardly see. So, Joseph brought his sons close to him, and his **father kissed them and embraced them.** 11 Israel said to Joseph, "I never expected to see your face again, and **now God has allowed me to see your children too."***

Verse 8—He **SAW** the sons—Acknowledging and seeing our grandchildren and children as unique and specially designed people solidifies their sense of personal value. They aren't just another member of the family. Call them by name and elevate their worth through personal attention.

Verse 8—He wanted to **KNOW** them—Every person is unique, with special gifts, personalities, and interests. Get to know your family. Ask questions, find out things that are specific to their interests.

Verse 9—He chose to **CONNECT** with them—It is often a choice that must be made to really connect with our grandchildren and children. Participate in their lives. Extend yourself beyond your own comfort zone.

Verse 9—He **BLESSED** them—In the next chapter we will discover the different elements of blessing, but let me say here that your responsibility for passing on blessing cannot and must not be overstated. The future and the encounters with God of your family members literally rests in your hands.

Verse 10—He expressed deep **AFFECTION** for them—Hugging, kissing, and jostling affectionately strengthens your family's personal identity and self worth. The pure affection that you offer to your grandchildren and children entrenches their personal security and self respect in a way that nothing or no one else can provide.

Verse 11—He Confirmed God's **LOVE** for them—Let your family hear from your own lips that God loves them, that Jesus died for them, and that nothing will ever separate them from that love.

You Are Needed

Understanding and embracing your role as the family patriarch is the first step in passing on God's blessing. It is imperative that you have a healthy perception of who you are and what your role is. If you are feeling restricted, it is important you get healed from the debilitation that hinders you. The Kingdom needs you now. Your family needs you now.

In the next chapter, we will discover the second step of the 5 step blueprint: the concepts of blessing in a practical and functional frame.

UNDERSTAND the POWER of BLESSING

Chapter 8 — STEP #2

Pray the Blessing of God into Their Lives

IN GENESIS 48, WHY WAS IT SO IMPORTANT THAT JOSEPH MADE IT TO HIS dad's bedside before his passing? What was the urgency? Beyond the emotional sentiment, was there something more that pushed Joseph to get to His father so quickly after hearing of his impending death?

I believe the answer to those questions can be addressed with one word—**BLESSING**. The blessing of God seems to be like a highly-valued treasure; something to be pursued, something to embrace that held tremendous personal significance. Esau, after learning of Jacob's theft of his rightful blessing, begged of his father in Genesis 27:38 " '... *do you have only one blessing, my father? Bless me, too, my father!' Then Esau wept aloud.*"

Esau had been deprived of something he obviously considered a deep loss. The denial of this seemingly priceless pronouncement was unquestionably important enough that it brought this big, burly, powerful man to tears. All players involved in this historic event realized that Isaac held the key to his son's destiny in a way that we, in our current culture, cannot fully grasp.

The transference of God's blessing from one generation to another is clearly recognized in Scripture as an exercise to be taken seriously and serves as an instrument to help craft the lives of those who receive it.

It is apparent that Joseph understood this reality and recognized that his father could impart something to his sons that no one else could to the same degree.

The entire scenario recorded in Genesis 48:1-4 speaks of urgency.

Some time later Joseph was told, "Your father is ill." So he took his two sons Manasseh and Ephraim along with him. When Jacob was told, "Your son Joseph has come to you," Israel rallied his strength and sat up on the bed. Jacob said to Joseph, "God Almighty appeared to me at Luz in the land of Canaan, and there he blessed me and said to me, 'I am going to make you fruitful and increase your numbers. I will make you a community of peoples, and I will give this land as an everlasting possession to your descendants after you.'

Joseph heard that his dad was dying, so he promptly took his sons to see him. Jacob heard Joseph was coming, so he instantly rallied his strength and got up to greet him. With no record of chit-chat, it seems Jacob immediately began to explain and communicate how Almighty God had blessed him over the years, and how those promises were pertinent for Joseph and his family. Joseph longed to receive from his father that blessing for his sons, and Jacob was well prepared to give that same blessing to his grandsons.

What Does The "Blessing" Really Mean?

The term or concept of BLESSING is spoken of over six hundred times in the Bible. The logical question, then, is what does it mean and how is it relevant to us as grandfathers and fathers for our families today?

In his work, *Theological Wordbook of the Old Testament*, John Oswalt defines the word **BLESSING** as, "To endue with power for success, prosperity, fecundity, longevity, etc. It conveys the idea of being strengthened, of our weakness being compensated for with God's strength."[11]

According to *Baker's Evangelical Dictionary of Biblical Theology*, the word **BLESS** connotes several important principles that can help us understand the value of passing blessing on to our own families.

"God's intention and desire to bless humanity is a central focus of his covenant relationships. For this reason, the concept of blessing pervades the biblical record. Two distinct ideas are present. First, a blessing was a public declaration of a favored status with God. Second, the blessing endowed power

[11] Oswalt, J. (1980). *Theological Wordbook of the Old Testament*. Chicago, IL: Moody Press.

for prosperity and success. ***In all cases, the blessing served as a guide and motivation to pursue a course of life within the blessing ...***

Three common themes are present in formal Old Testament blessings. ***First, the greater blesses the lesser****, a fact picked up by the writer of Hebrews to demonstrate the superiority of Melchizedek to Abraham (Heb 7:6-7).* ***Second, the blessing is a sign of special favor*** *that is intended to result in prosperity and success (Deu 28:3-7).* ***Third, the blessing is actually an invocation for God's blessing:*** *"May God Almighty bless you and make you fruitful" (Gen 28:3)."*[12]

The first record we have in the Bible of the word **BLESS** is found in Genesis 1:20-22.

And God said, "Let the water teem with living creatures, and let birds fly above the earth across the vault of the sky." So God created the great creatures of the sea and every living thing with which the water teems and that moves about in it, according to their kinds, and every winged bird according to its kind. And God saw that it was good. ***God blessed them and said, "Be fruitful and increase*** *in number and fill the water in the seas, and let the birds increase on the earth."*

When God created His first living beings, He added an instruction and an enablement that is repeated over and over again throughout the Scriptures. **"Be fruitful and increase ..."** It is the intent of God that all His creation be blessed and prosper as He enables.

---

[12]Elwell, W.A., (1996). *Baker's Evangelical Dictionary of Biblical Theology*. Grand Rapids, MI: Baker Books.

God's Intended Purpose for Passing on Blessing

Why is the **BLESSING** so important? The Scriptures give dozens of examples of the blessing of God being imparted to individuals and the obvious value that is placed on the exercise. What is it that God causes to happen when His blessing is pronounced on a person? There are far too many examples in the Bible of one generation passing blessing to the next to ignore or miss the significance of this powerful experience.

When I personally pick up my grandchildren with the intention of imparting God's blessing into their lives, I am doing so with a clear understanding that by my obedience to the Lord in this manner, I will be accomplishing something in them for the rest of their lives. I am convinced I am serving as a conduit of God's desire for their lives. That which I am exercising in the seen world is, in fact, releasing something extremely powerful

> I would be grossly negligent to not embrace this responsibility and stand in as the patriarch on behalf of every member of my family

in the unseen world. When I bless my grandchildren and children, God, the entire angelic realm, and all the forces of darkness are witnessing the establishment of the Lordship of Christ in the lives of each of them. It is a life altering, Kingdom establishing, darkness shattering event. I would be grossly negligent to not embrace this responsibility and stand in as the patriarch on behalf of every member of my family, both in the present tense and for the generations that will follow.

That being said, what is actually happening when I pass on blessing? If, when I pray over my family members, I am expecting results, for what can

I hope and believe God? I have listed ten things I believe happen when we pray the blessing of God over our families.

1) INVOKES GOD'S AUTHORITY FOR THE PURPOSE OF PROSPERING

This is the root meaning of the concept of blessing. All that we have, all that we are, and all that we hope for, is God's to give. When I pray over my grandchildren and my children, I am doing so in the Name of Jesus, recognizing that in His Name all blessings flow. I want to release into my family's lives the power of God. I want to expect and believe that they will live in the realm of His Kingdom and that He will give watch over them every day of their lives. I am speaking, invoking that authority into their world with the expectation that the authority of Jesus will accompany them at every juncture of their life. I am believing that because I have been faithful in passing on this blessing, they will have things happen on their behalf without them even realizing that it is God working mysteriously in their corner.

2) CREATES A HEALTHY SPIRITUAL PASSAGEWAY INTO THE HEART OF THE ONE BEING BLESSED

There is a constant battle for the souls and lives of every human being. The enemy never quits trying to "steal, kill and destroy" (John 10:10), but thank the Lord Jesus that His Holy Spirit is ever drawing and leading the hearts of our families to Himself. I call this phenomenon "the arrested moment" in a person's journey toward Christ. It is that moment in a person's life when suddenly, there comes a keen and defining revelation of God's grace and His incredible love for that individual; the moment a response to Jesus is so real it cannot be explained or denied. It is that moment that you know this could only be God.

There are many hindrances on a person's road to discovering the grace of God. When we pray the blessing of God over that person's life, we are in truth, blocking out some of those forces preventing the experience from happening. We are helping to pave the way for them to have an open heart to Jesus' love.

As the patriarchs in our families, we play an instrumental role in establishing that passageway. In some ways, it authorizes the ongoing revelation of Christ's love and redemption to the next generation. It takes place in the Spirit, and is a principle clearly articulated in the Scriptures. It is one that places much onus on us as grandfathers and fathers.

3) AFFIRMS CHRIST'S LEADERSHIP

When we pray the blessing of God over someone, we are, in essence, telling them that it is right, wise, and good to allow Jesus to be Lord of their lives; we are assuring them that it is ok. There is so much negativity people must wade through when it comes to their walk with Jesus that when they hear someone with a degree of authority in their life speak words of blessing, it creates a liberating sense of attachment to the Lordship of Christ. In effect, you are creating a bond with Jesus on their behalf. That bond is emotional, intellectual, and spiritual. Faith comes by hearing the Word of God. The Word is Spirit and ignites spiritual realities in our lives when we hear it.

The Lordship of Jesus is what guides us to the freedom of truth. It is what gives us the confidence that He is good and that He never leaves us nor forsakes us. His Lordship is what moves people to become world changers and dynamic men and women of God. It is His Lordship that allows us to trust and walk in obedience despite opposition and challenges to our faith and courage. The submission to

Christ's Lordship is what sets us apart as believers and defines who we are as servants in His Kingdom.

4) INVOKES GOD'S FAVOR

Quite literally, we are speaking God's favor into the lives of our families in harmony with His Word. The Word of God is full of His promises for us as believers. Those promises reflect His favor. When we speak blessing into the lives of our grandchildren and children, we are being obedient to His Word and are alerting their lives to those promises for themselves.

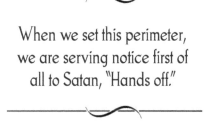

When we set this perimeter, we are serving notice first of all to Satan, "Hands off."

The favor of God is a familiar theme in the Scriptures and is often prayed for and promised to those that walk in faithfulness to Christ. The very word **BLESSING** implies God's favor. As the family patriarch, I am speaking this favor into and onto the lives of my family. By invoking this favor into their lives, we are binding the promises to them as spiritual benefactors.

5) ESTABLISHES SPIRITUAL PERIMETERS

I have been told that cowboys of old carried with them a rope woven from horsehair. The rope was used at night to create a large circle on the ground in which they would then set their sleeping blankets. Snakes and other night crawlers would not cross over the horse hair, allowing the cowboys to have a restful sleep, unafraid of any unwanted vermin attacks while they slept. The Bible speaks of a *hedge of thorns* surrounding the children of God for their protection from assaults of the enemy.

When we pray the blessing of God into the lives of our family members, we are setting a perimeter around them in the spirit as well. The encroachment of the enemy and the tendency to wander both pose a threat to the well-being of our grandchildren and children. It is my conviction that when we set this perimeter, we are serving notice first of all to Satan, "Hands off." We are establishing spiritual covering and protection for them. We are declaring to the powers of darkness that this person belongs to Jesus and they have no right or jurisdiction over them.

Secondly, I believe when we pray God's blessing over our family, we are determining boundaries for them to stay within themselves. My mother used to remind me as a kid, to "be sure your sins will find you out." That little phrase haunted me while I was living outside of what I knew to be truth. Regardless of whether you quote such an ominous verse in your prayer or not, the principle and reality of the guiding influence of the Holy Spirit is ever present.

6) ESTABLISHES SPIRITUAL CONTINUITY FROM GENERATION TO GENERATION

As I've already established in detail in a previous chapter, the continuation of spiritual connectedness from generation to generation is clearly a reality. That which my forefathers held to in their faith a few hundred years ago has become a personal ideologue in my own life. Their love for Jesus is my passion also. Their desire to see the world impacted for Christ is my desire as well.

I know my longing to experience and know Jesus in deeper ways will find its way through the corridors of the Spirit into the lives of my grandchildren, great-grandchildren, great-great-grandchildren, and for generations beyond. What a magnificent hope.

7) ACKNOWLEDGES AND CONFIRMS DEPENDENCY ON GOD AS PROVIDER, LEADER, AND CREATOR

By declaring in Jesus' Name that He is the source of all we have and all we are, we are confirming in the hearts of our family that whenever they are in need, it is God to whom they will turn. This confirmation and acknowledgment reassures them that Jesus cares, is intimately involved in their lives, and that He can and will do for them those things they never dreamed or expected could happen.

8) VALIDATES THE UNIQUENESS AND IDENTITY OF THE INDIVIDUAL

One of the most manipulative tactics of Satan against our grandchildren and children is the assault against their personal identity. In our present culture, our young people are constantly being subjected to images and messages questioning their self worth and suggesting they could be much more popular, or much less inadequate, if they would just subscribe to a different product or style. Even though that has always been a challenge while discovering who you are as a young person, the advent of increased and elaborate commercialism has made it even more difficult in today's modern world of technology.

A more diabolical attack is currently placing the youngest generation of today in the crosshairs of the enemy—sexual confusion and sexual orientation. There is incredible pressure today for society to capitulate to the barrage of messages to not hold clear and strong alliances with the way God has created you as a person. Boys are boys and girls are girls. Whoever thought our society would so quickly digress into a Sodom and Gomorrah mentality? This is a spiritual battle which can only be won in a spiritual fight.

When praying the blessing of God into your family's lives, speak truth to them and reaffirm them in who God has created them to be. They are fearfully and wonderfully made. God, by His Spirit, brings confidence and internal witness to who we are as individuals. It comes through the revelation of who we are in Christ. That revelation is part of what we believe God for when we impart His blessing into the lives of our grandchildren and children.

Each member of your family has their own unique gifts, talents, and personalities. That uniqueness must be encouraged and supported as they submit themselves to God for His ongoing development and leadership toward a rich and full life in Christ.

9) STIMULATES VISION FOR THE COURSE OF THEIR LIVES

In the natural, we are often a product of our environment. It is common for someone to grow into the kind of person or even into the vocation represented by those they were most closely associated with growing up. We develop objectives and vision largely based on the influences of others. Likewise, our family members are also significantly influenced by the words people have spoken to them or over them at pivotal times in their lives.

> Jacob, in Genesis 49, had a prophetic word for each of his sons

In a spiritual manner, our sons and daughters can be profoundly impacted and influenced when a prophetic word or directive word is shared with them during the exercise of praying blessings over their lives. Jacob, in Genesis 49, had a prophetic word for each of his sons. Some words were positive and some not so much, but he clearly articulated his understanding of the direction their lives would take in the years to come.

When praying blessing over my grandchildren, I want to hear the Word of the Lord for them and cast vision into their souls in a way that will contribute to the direction in which they will live their lives.

10) CONNECTS THE LIVES OF THE *BLESSER* AND THE *BLESSEE*

There is something powerful that happens between people when they pray for one another. There is something significant that takes place when grampa or dad lays hands on their grandchildren or children and speaks the blessing of God into their lives. There is a bond that is forged in the Spirit that is unbreakable. It is difficult to explain but very real nevertheless. It is memorable and it is monumental. That indelible image of receiving something being passed on from God is etched into the heart of the individual in a life-altering manner. It can only be explained as a "God thing," powerful and precious.

The 5 Elements of Blessing

I have many times heard it said that men aren't sure what to say or what to do when it comes time to serve in a patriarchal way and speak the blessing of God over their families. In some ways that is a sad indictment of us as men, but mostly I get it. It is because of this lack of understanding that I looked at the Scriptures to try to condense the principles of blessing down to a manageable and memorable presentation for men to use. After reading and rereading many of the biblical examples of blessings, I have assembled what I believe to be five elements or categories that cover most of the recorded accounts of blessing in the Scriptures.

The purpose of these five elements of blessing is to create a tool that can be easily and effectively used to guide men through the process of this second step. If you are a little uncertain about what to pray over your family, these five categories will assist you and lead you through a meaningful experience with your grandchildren or children.

I highly recommend that you commit these five elements to memory and be prepared to express them continually in your private prayer time, in one-on-one encounters with your family, or in an open ceremony designed to publicly impart the patriarchal blessing on your sons' and daughters' lives.

What are the five elements?

1) The **KNOWLEDGE** of God

The greatest thing we can pray over our family members is that they would know Jesus in a deep and personal manner. It doesn't help our kids if they just know *about* Jesus through stories and Sunday school lessons. The only real strength they will gain spiritually is when they know Jesus for themselves in a powerful, life-altering way.

Ephesians 1:17-19
"*I keep asking that the God of our Lord Jesus Christ, the glorious Father, may give you the Spirit of wisdom and revelation, so that you may know him better. I pray that the eyes of your heart may be enlightened in order that you may know the hope to which he has*

called you, the riches of his glorious inheritance in his holy people, and his incomparably great power for us who believe."

2) The **POWER** of God

There is a deeper and more significant level of anointing and authority in Christ when we walk in the fulness of His power in the Holy Spirit. It must be our desire and place to pray that our grandchildren and children would be filled with the Holy Spirit and that they would experience the power of God in a way that would elevate their effectiveness in His Kingdom.

Acts 1:8
"But you will receive power when the Holy Spirit comes on you; and you will be my witnesses in Jerusalem, and in all Judea and Samaria, and to the ends of the earth."

Acts 4:33
"With great power the apostles continued to testify to the resurrection of the Lord Jesus. And God's grace was so powerfully at work in them all ..."

3) The **FAVOR** of God

The favor of God encompasses much of what we consider material and natural provisions and blessings. I suggest when you pray, you categorize the favor of God in the following ways:
- ✦ Health
- ✦ Wealth and finances
- ✦ Relationships and family
- ✦ Protective covering from anything that may come against them

3 John 2 (NKJV)

"Beloved, I pray that you may prosper in all things and be in health, just as your soul prospers."

Psalm 1:3

"That person is like a tree planted by streams of water, which yields its fruit in season and whose leaf does not wither— whatever they do prospers."

Psalm 5:11

"But let all who take refuge in you be glad; let them ever sing for joy. Spread your protection over them, that those who love your name may rejoice in you. Surely, LORD, you bless the righteous; you surround them with your favor as with a shield."

4) The **PURPOSE** of God

One of the great discoveries as a child of God is when we figure out what unique call and purpose God has placed on our lives. Every individual has a unique role to play in Kingdom service. As the patriarch in our family, we can play an instrumental role in praying for this revelation to become a reality in the lives of our grandchildren and children. To speak encouragement or prophetically can create a desire within a child to want to serve the Lord in a powerful and meaningful way.

Matthew 9:37-38

"Then he said to his disciples, "The harvest is plentiful but the workers are few. Ask the Lord of the harvest, therefore, to send out workers into his harvest field."

Romans 12:5-6

"... so, in Christ we, though many, form one body, and each member belongs to all the others. We have different gifts, according to the grace given to each of us ..."

5) The **DESIGN** of God

The self image a child or young person has of themselves forms a critical part of who they believe they can be in a complex world. There are many mixed and confusing messages they must filter as they seek to grapple with their identity. A right word and a healthy image spoken by the right person at the right time can set the course for that individual's entire life. If you couple that with the revelation that comes from the Holy Spirit on how precious and loved each person is, you can witness the development of a powerful man or woman of God right before your eyes.

Psalm 139:13-16

"For you created my inmost being; you knit me together in my mother's womb. I praise you because I am fearfully and wonderfully made; your works are wonderful, I know that full well. My frame was not hidden from you when I was made in the secret place, when I was woven together in the depths of the earth. Your eyes saw my unformed body; all the days ordained for me were written in your book before one of them came to be."

The High 5 Blessing

At one of our workshops, as a group we were discussing diverse ways we could use to remember the five elements of blessing and then use them in practical ways with our families. One of the young gentlemen (interestingly enough, neither a grandfather nor a father) who was attending, came up with a brilliant idea that has stuck and been used effectively all over the country now. We nicknamed it the "High 5 Blessing."

I'm sure most everyone is familiar with the ritual of giving a "High 5" to your children or grandchildren. Usually when I offer a high 5 to my grandson, he feels inspired to punch me in the stomach, but that is a story for another day. The idea behind the "High 5 Blessing" is to memorize each of the five elements of blessing and assign the individual element to one of your five fingers. When you have opportunity to place your hand on the recipient of blessing, you can quickly and deliberately pronounce that blessing on their life. Each time you make contact with your family member—son, daughter, or grandchild—you can be imparting that blessing on them.

In the following chapter, we will talk about step #3—**The laying on of hands** and the power associated with it. Using the High 5 Blessing accompanied by a greater understanding of the transference of blessing through the laying on of hands can equip you with powerful Kingdom tools to set the course of a young person's life.

LAY HANDS on THEM

Chapter 9   STEP #3

Transfer Blessing by Laying Hands on Them

IT HAD BEEN A LONG DAY. IN FACT, IT HAD BEEN A LONG COUPLE OF WEEKS. They had walked as a group for miles in the heat and dust of the Middle Eastern countryside. There had been an incredible number of experiences that could not be explained sufficiently unless you had been there to witness them for yourself. The instruction, the parables, the pure divine insights were nothing short of celestial revelation. These simple, hardworking men had been handpicked and subjected to such profound manifestations and eternally charged interactions that they really couldn't be blamed for being somewhat overwhelmed with the whole journey to date. It seems reasonable to assume that the disciples of Jesus were trying to process so much in such a short period of time that there had to have been a large degree of sensory overload.

Peter, James, and John, especially had witnessed things that could only be listed in the "beyond human comprehension" category. They were with Jesus on the Mount of Transfiguration only a couple of weeks earlier and were eyewitnesses to the unbelievable glory of God overshadowing Jesus, watching as His very countenance and clothing became brilliant, heavenly white, radiating the power and light of God right before them. They saw and listened as Moses and Elijah appeared with Jesus just a few feet away. They heard the thunderous majestic voice of Almighty God proclaim, "This is my Son in whom I am well pleased." They could only stand breathless and in awe as they were allowed a peek behind the Kingdom veil. What they witnessed, what they experienced had never been observed before and would never be seen on earth again. Imagine their emotions. Try to put yourself in their thought process. The whole experience had to have been nothing short of mind blowing for average laymen such as these guys. Oh ya, one more thing. As they came down from the mountain, Jesus gave them an instruction: "Guys, don't tell anybody about any of this. You have to keep it a secret."

What? Thanks a lot. They had just witnessed the most spectacular event in history, and they were supposed to just sit on it and not tell anybody. The excitement and adrenaline must have been incredible. They had to have been supercharged with both feelings and questions, and really, could you blame them if they were feeling just a little self important?

For days, the journey took them from city to city, listening intently to this magnificent man as He taught eternal truths about the Scriptures and about Himself. This small band of select men were riveted to every word Jesus uttered. Their jaws must have dropped each time a Pharisee came along with a new challenge regarding the law, trying to trip up this profoundly intuitive Rabbi, only to have Him turn the truth on them, sending them away frustrated and angry again and again. Demonstrations of miracles, healing, and demons being cast out were evident, day after day, city after city, and crowd after crowd.

As word spread and the crowds grew, I can only speculate that there may have been lots of highly influential people, and maybe even local celebrities, all hoping to get in on the excitement. Human nature would suggest that it's possible the disciples faced the emotional intersect of feeling self important and understandably protective of Jesus as they did their best to navigate through throngs of people. Just months earlier they were nobodies; simple fisherman and tradesmen. What a ride.

Those were the days and hours leading up to this moment. Mile after mile and stop after stop, the disciples went back and forth between being security guards and students, knowing they were literally Jesus' inner circle. I can't help but think protecting Him and maintaining their inner circle status were foremost on their minds.

I'm sure it seemed logical for them to chase people away when they were bringing their young children into the crowd, trying to get close to Jesus. After all, the disciples had been observing Jesus bring very influential, highly educated, and well respected people to a point of being speechless with His wisdom and stature. They watched as local politicians and religious leaders were stood up to and put in their place with rebuttals no one would ever have dared to attempt. That's what Jesus was doing and He was really good at it. How would He have time for or interest in some kid? Did these people not know who He was? Or maybe they wondered if the people knew who they were? Whatever they thought, they obviously concluded that Jesus would not be willing to give these children His attention.

Poor guys. They couldn't have been more wrong; Jesus had yet another surprise for them.

Jesus' Contact With the Children

Mark 10:13-16 (PME)

*Then some people came to him **bringing little children for him to touch**. The disciples tried to **discourage them**. When Jesus saw this, **he was indignant** and told them, "You must let little children come to me—never stop them! For the **kingdom of God belongs** to such as these. Indeed, I assure you that the man who does not accept the kingdom of God like a little child will never enter it." Then he took the children **in his arms and laid his hands on them and blessed them.***

This simple four verse story is packed with insights and wisdom relevant to us today as the patriarchs in our own families. While it's true the fundamental message of the text is that people must have the faith and openness of a child to be able to understand entrance to the Kingdom of God, there is much more we need to learn from Jesus and His handling of the people involved. It is very significant and relevant to note that there are three points of physical contact spoken of in this much-loved account.

<u>**Point of contact 1**</u>—Families bringing their children to Jesus hoping that *He might touch them* (verse 13).

<u>**Point of contact 2**</u>—*He took them in His arms*. One translation reads *He embraced them* and yet another says *He hugged them* (verse 16).

<u>**Point of contact 3**</u>—*He laid hands on them and Blessed them* (verse 16).

By stretching your imagination a little, it's possible to make the argument that a fourth point of contact could have happened as well.

Point of contact 4—*When Jesus saw this, He was indignant with them* (verse 14).

This last point of contact might have been Jesus giving His disciples a swift kick in the backside for missing such an important reality! However, since the text doesn't actually say that, we will leave it be.

The physical connection between Jesus and the children cannot be overlooked. It is well documented that Jesus encouraged the children to come to Him and when they did, He went beyond a passing, "Hi, how are you?" kind of introduction. The children clearly felt safe with Him and the parents believed His *touch* would have some kind of profound impact.

In this story, there are also five key observations that need to be made to better understand the value of the third step in the 5 step blueprint.

Five Key Observations

1. The Opposition

The story is told of Walt Disney that whenever he had a new idea for a story, an attraction, or character, if his team did not immediately oppose him, he would not follow through with the project. His reasoning was that it wasn't far-reaching enough if everyone initially agreed, and was therefore not worth pursuing. Whether the story of Walt Disney is fact or fiction, the moral of the story is true.

Every road to significance will be pitted against the potholes of opposition. Discouragement, hostility, animosity, or even blatant resistance are the norm when we follow any pathway to fruitfulness. The Bible aptly articulates that Satan's agenda is designed to defeat, or at least impair, the work of God in our lives and the journey toward a full experience with Christ. *"He has come to kill, steal, and destroy"* (John 10:10).

It's interesting to note that the disciples were just doing what comes naturally when something beyond the norm presents itself. They were not expecting these kids to be pushing their way into the crowd. Whether the opposition was inspired by spiritual forces of darkness or not, is irrelevant. The issue is that Jesus' disciples were impeding a work which God wanted to do, and He insisted they stand down.

Here are the facts for us today. God is passionate about children and deeply desires to bless them. It is our mandate to serve as the conduit of that blessing and we must not succumb to pressures and oppositions that emerge and raise their ugly head, seeking to prevent us from this eternally valuable mission.

As established in an earlier chapter, Satan has been systematically and strategically scheming to immobilize men in their role as the heads of their families, their communities, their churches, and our nations. There has been a concerted spiritual assault on headship and the place of the patriarch. This is by design and can be confirmed by simply observing what is going on in our present-day culture. There is a general fear of men, especially when it comes to their relationship with children. I readily admit that it is too often justified. However, when analyzed proportionately, the numbers are skewed to the point that no man is to be trusted. It is sad and unfortunate that so many men have been rendered emotionally impotent because of this opposition. Loss of relationship, loss of affection, and fear of physical contact with our grandchildren and children are the result of the lies of our spiritual enemies and their misguided messengers.

"Humble yourselves, resist the devil and he will flee from you" (James 4:7 NLT).

Guys, it's time to be men. Don't allow yourself to be pushed back. Stand up to the opposition and engage in the mandate to which God has called you.

2. <u>Jesus Insisted the Children Come to Him</u>

Without chasing down this story in too much detail, I think it is worth noting a couple of important points. First of all, Jesus **defined access** to the Kingdom through the children and was **indignant** with the disciples for hindering them from coming to Him. He immediately reprimanded His students for their lack of understanding. It was as though His followers had not been paying attention to what He had been saying all along. Jesus immediately and forcefully took advantage of the moment to establish the value of the children and their innocent and trusting souls. Not only did He understand that these young ones were the future of His Kingdom message, but more importantly, He saw into their hearts and knew that the openness and tender receptivity of a child were what was required of all mankind to experience what Jesus was offering. The doorway to the Kingdom of God could only be opened by the simple faith of a child.

Secondly, the parents **brought** those kids to Jesus. They knew if they could get close to Him, there would be some kind of God-induced favor available to their children. I love the persistence of the parents. They were giving Jesus permission to place His divine approval on their little lives. Unless a person is in an unhealthy state of mind, everyone wants the absolute best for their family. These parents saw an opportunity to get their children close to God, and they weren't about to pass it up—even if it meant fighting off the security guards!

As family patriarchs, we have been commissioned by God to represent Him in the Name of Jesus, by bringing the children to Him today. Preventing them or denying them is completely unacceptable. Jesus is as indignant today about hindering the children as He was on that day, and our mandate is no less crucial. *"Do not forbid them for the Kingdom belongs to people like these."*

3. He Embraced Them

As indicated earlier, different translations use different words to describe the contact Jesus had with the children. I especially like the one which says, "He hugged them" (CEB). Regardless of how you read it, the image is the same. Jesus gathered the children around Him and hugged them, jostled with them, gave them noogies, and generally made them each feel as if they were the most important human beings on the entire earth.

Verse 13 shows not only the heart of Jesus for the children, but it indicates the longing of the parents for their children. The parents continued to press in toward Jesus, *"So that He could **touch them.**"* I love that phrase.

When my daughter, Tiffany, was around eight years old, she taught me a lesson about the longing of a child that I have never forgotten. I was driving her to school one morning, following the same routine we followed every morning. I would be mindlessly driving, focusing on one of a hundred things that required my attention that day, oblivious to the eight-year-old little girl sitting behind me equally disengaged in the familiar surroundings of our daily ride, quietly reading her book. She always sat in the middle of the back seat between her two older brothers. From the minute she got into the vehicle, she would open a book and not lift her head until we arrived at the school. Morning after morning the ride was the same; very little conversation and very little distraction from her reading. It's pretty easy as a parent to miss opportunities when your children are quietly preoccupied with other things. This particular morning, however, she changed my thinking and my life forever with one simple, innocent request.

I remember the scene vividly. I was driving with my left hand on the steering wheel and my right arm resting on the back of the front seat. My arm, therefore, was directly in front of where Tiffany was seated. Without raising her little blonde head and without losing focus of her book, she spontaneously said, **"Daddy, will you touch me?"**

Her lips were making an innocent request, but her heart was shouting a longing deep within her being. She was saying, *Daddy show me you love me, reaffirm your protection over me, show me that you notice me and that I am important to you. Let me know we are friends and that I matter more to you than anything else in the world.* My heart melted and to this day, whenever I am with Tiff or one of my boys, I hug them as much as I can. I want them to know without me having to say anything, that everything Tiffany was expressing that day is true and more.

In his article *"Hands on Research: The Science of Touch,"*[13] Dacher Keltner makes some interesting observations of about the power of touch, as shared on the following page.

---

[13] Keltner, C. (2010). *Hands on Research: The Science of Touch.* Retrieved from https://www.plpit.com/hands-on-research-the-science-of-toucharticle-by-dacher-keltner-2010read-the-full-article/

"In recent years, a wave of studies have documented some incredible emotional and physical benefits that come from touch. This research is suggesting that touch is truly fundamental to human communication, bonding and health.

The benefits start from the moment we're born. A review of research, conducted by Tiffany Field, a leader in the field of touch, found that preterm newborns who receive just three 15-minute sessions of touch therapy each day for 5-10 days gained 47 percent more weight than premature infants who'd received standard medical treatment.

This research sheds light on why, historically, an overwhelming percentage of babies in orphanages where the caretakers starved them of touch have failed to grow to their expected height and weight, and have shown behavioral problems.

"To touch can be to give life," said Michelangelo, and he was absolutely right.

From this frontier of touch research, we know thanks to the neuroscientific Edmond Rolls, that touch activates the brain's orbitofrontal cortex, which is linked to feelings of reward and compassion.

There are studies showing that touch signals safety and trust; it soothes. Basic warm touch calms cardiovascular stress. It activates the body's vagus nerve, which is intimately involved with our compassionate response, and a simple touch can trigger a release of oxytocin, aka, "the love hormone."

In a study by Jim Coan and Richard Davidson, participants laying in an MRI brain scanner, anticipating a painful blast of white noise, showed heightened brain activity in regions associated with threat and stress. But participants whose romantic partner stroked their arm while they waited, didn't show this reaction at all. Touch had turned off the threat switch."

There is a reason Satan wants to mess up the intimate relationships within families and the joy of affectionate touch between parents and gramparents with their children. Meaningful and sincere physical contact is a powerful conduit for communicating the love of God and the acceptance of an individual by their Savior. The more pure, unadulterated affection shown to a child, the more likely they are to be able to receive the love that God has for them.

4. <u>He laid hands on them</u>

When I read this part of the passage, I immediately see how the intent of Jesus changes. Initially, I see a picture of Jesus playfully communicating with the children by hugging them and having them sit on His knee, learning their names and identifying which family group they came with. I can see the proud parents smiling and pointing, mom and dad holding one another with deep satisfaction that their little one could get close to this amazing man. The text doesn't tell us the length of this interaction, but there is a distinct shift in behavior at some point.

Jesus went from hugging, to a much more intentional and purposeful display of action. The Bible says He laid His hands on them and blessed them. I'm not entirely sure what this transition of intent looked like, but I believe the interaction had a two-fold purpose. One was to show acceptance, and the second was to impart the power and favor of God on their lives. The fact that the text specifically denotes that Jesus *placed His hands on them*, signifies the importance and the value of the expression.

I believe Jesus' very countenance would have changed, recognizing that the lives of those children needed God's favor on them and that this was no small or frivolous matter. He was, in fact, setting the very course of their lives.

Biblical Purposes for the Laying on of Hands

The practice of laying hands on people and then imparting God's intentions is a common theme in the Bible throughout the Old and New Testaments. When we follow this powerful principle, we are keeping the integrity of the Scriptures and we therefore must be faithful and obedient in applying the practice according to His Word.

A Fundamental Doctrine

"... the elementary teachings about Christ ... the laying on of hands ... " (Hebrews 6:1-2)

Healing

"... the people brought to Jesus all who had various kinds of sickness, and laying his hands on each one, he healed them" (Luke 4:40).

Receiving the Holy Spirit

"Then Peter and John placed their hands on them, and they received the Holy Spirit" (Acts 8:17).

Impartation of Spiritual Gifts

"Do not neglect your gift, which was given you through prophecy when the body of elders laid their hands on you" 1 Timothy 4:14.

Commissioning for Ministry

"So after they had fasted and prayed, they placed their hands on them and sent them off" (Acts 13:3).

Blessing

"And he took the children in his arms, placed his hands on them and blessed them" (Mark 10:16).

Extension Cord of Power

When I look for metaphors to define and describe the exercise of laying hands on someone to pray for them, I always think of an extension cord. The cord is a conduit of power from the source to the appliance. In and of itself the cord is nothing more than a tool. The source is the power. The energy and the electricity reside in that source. The appliance or the recipient requires the electricity to fulfill its intended purpose. Unless there is a means to which to connect the source, that appliance is of little value. When the extension cord is plugged into both the source and the appliance, you have a completed circuit that releases the power in a way that maximizes the contribution of each component.

My dad used to tell a story about his younger days. He grew up on the farm, and by all accounts, was very much a prankster and a mischievous boy. As a farm kid, he was always around animals and developed a fondness and familiarity for them. He loved the cows and the horses but was not crazy about the chickens, and he definitely didn't like the pigs. The story I remember most about his dislike for the pigs was how he would introduce them to the new technology of the day—the electric fence. I can still see my dad telling the story with a wry grin on his face as he remembered the experience as if it was still a fresh source of personal pleasure.

The pigs would be wallowing around squealing and wrestling as only a pig can do in an area of the yard they weren't to be. Dad would be given the responsibility of redirecting them back to their assigned pen, which, if you know anything about pigs, is not necessarily a simple task. He seemed to enjoy it most when the pigs were camped out near the electric fence, making it possible for him to wade into the middle of them, take a pig by the leg, reach across, and grab onto the highly-charged fence. As you can imagine, the electrical surge would go from the fence through dad like an extension cord, and into the unsuspecting pig. With a jolt, a screech, and a kick, the pig would go high-tailing it out of the area back toward the barn where it belonged— farming techniques at their finest. What an innovator my dad was.

When you lay hands on your grandchildren or children as the patriarch of your family, you serve as the extension cord between the power of God and the value of the children. It is your opportunity and responsibility to be plugged into God and then lay hands on your family with the expressed purpose of transferring His power and favor into their lives so they can become everything He wants them to be.

3 Ways to Practice the "Laying on of Hands" Principle

I realize that grampas will have greater or lesser access to their grandchildren. It's not always expedient, practical, or convenient to lay hands on family members, so I offer some simple suggestions depending on your circumstances.

Do it Privately: If you can't actually be in the same room at the same time with your family members, I suggest getting a photograph of them and laying hands on it. An actual picture or one on your phone would work. Or, a letter or text from them can be used if that is your only contact with them. God is bigger than all impediments and looks on your heart and motivation. Your faithful prayer will bear much fruit.

Do it Personally: Find times and occasions when you can physically lay hands on your grandchildren and children. Being present and involved is a powerful, life-altering privilege and responsibility. Do not shy away. Lay your hands on them and impart the blessing of God on them.

Do it Publicly: Ceremonies are a powerful way to establish and entrench eternal truths into the lives of children. The Jewish culture celebrates with many different festivals; the Bar Mitzvah and Bat Mitzvah are two of the most important. Public displays of recognition and deep personal acknowledgments of the individual make the experience profoundly important in the life-journey of the young boy or girl.

As Christians, we need to learn to celebrate the life of the child, but more importantly, the power of God and the desire of our living God to impact that child's journey with Him.

Family celebrations, church festivals, community gatherings, and many other opportunities can lend to these special occasions.

5. He Blessed Them

In Genesis 48 we learned that Joseph recognized his dad had something no one else could give to his children—the patriarch's blessing. I don't need to restate the importance of this event, but I do want to make it clear that Jesus didn't just have playtime with the children. He gathered them together, He laid hands on them, and He BLESSED them. The obvious transition and emphasis of this part of the story make abundantly clear the value and significance God places on the exercise of blessing.

As the old saying goes, *if it's good enough for Jesus, it's good enough for me.* Do it!

SPEAK WORDS of LIFE OVER THEM

Chapter 10   STEP #4

Activate the Spirit of God
Through the Spoken Word

AS A KID, I LIVED TO PLAY HOCKEY. MY DAD WAS AN EXCELLENT ATHLETE, and I'd watch him play and think, *Someday, I will be a player also*. As a farm kid, my siblings and I would skate on anything that resembled ice: a snowy road, runoff from the water trough for the livestock, sloughs, dugouts, and occasionally the outdoor skating arena in our local town. It was pure fun and a joy to skate and play the game, but it was just a game. I became fairly proficient at it as I grew older and opportunities opened for me to play at very competitive levels. Junior hockey in Western Canada in those days was considered elite and prestigious, and that's to what I aspired. At home, everyone was encouraging and complimentary of my abilities and passion to play. It became a part of my identity and I experienced nothing but support and a certain degree of respect.

I learned a lot about people and human nature when I moved away to play hockey. I discovered that many, if not most people, and especially those who have a level of authority and control, have a limited understanding of how to influence and lead others. In those days, no one studied sport psychology or leadership principles, so they led from insecurities and limited knowledge of both people and the game itself. The people of whom I speak were "coaches." A great majority of them were (and I will be kind), clueless. They believed that intimidation, belittlement, and harsh criticism were how to get the most from an athlete's contributions and skills. I had never experienced being berated and made to feel incompetent, incapable, and insignificant like I did from those men.

My confidence and self-esteem diminished rapidly, and all but disappeared. Within a short time, my love for the game had vanished. I hated it. The people who controlled the game had systematically reduced my perception of myself and my abilities as a player and more importantly, as a person, on a scale of one-to-ten, to about a three. To be clear, it wasn't unique to me in any way. They spoke the same way to everyone except their chosen stars. It was as much their attitudes as their words, making the culture around the game excessively negative. Being yelled at and embarrassed in front of teammates was a normal and seemingly acceptable means of communication. Everyone learned to tolerate it, but for me it created deep self-doubt and insecurity.

After playing several years, I learned to endure the criticism as a part of life. After all, as I was once told, "That's just hockey." In those years I had limited success and often found myself floundering just to make a team or to be given limited playing time. I had been told many times

What we say, how we say it, when we say it, and to whom we say it, matters

how incapable I was, so it must have been true.

Season after season I would try to make the next level, with my ultimate goal to play in the highest Junior league in the world—the Western Hockey League, or as it was affectionately known, "The Dub." When the day came I was told I had finally made a team and had reached my much sought-after dream, I received the news with limited enthusiasm and a large degree of skepticism. My experiences of the previous few years had made me keenly aware of the potential disappointment.

In previous seasons, if I made even a small mistake on the ice, it would have resulted in disparaging criticism and prolonged periods of lost ice time. It's what I expected, and it was what I got.

It was in the first game of a new season, playing at the highest level I had ever played, that it happened. The atmosphere was intimidating yet exhilarating. I couldn't believe I was actually there, on the ice ready for opening face off, in front of several thousand people. It was everything I had imagined and more. To be honest I was probably thinking, *Don't screw this up.*

As a defenseman, there are certain plays that are absolute cardinal rules. They cannot be broken or you will most likely create scoring opportunities for the opposition. So there I was, the first shift of the first game in my long-sought-after dream league. Off the opening face-off, the puck went behind my net. I retreated to pick it up. As in many things in life, my intentions were good, but my execution was poor. When I came out from behind my own net on the lefthand side, I spotted one of my teammates on the right-hand side out by our team's blue line. This is where one of those cardinal rules of hockey was broken. I attempted to pass the puck in front of my own net across the ice to the awaiting forward, so he could advance the play up the ice. There was only one problem. A highly skilled opponent happened to be standing in front of my net in-between me and my mate. The opposing player promptly intercepted my attempted pass and quickly shot it into our team's net. Oops. A few seconds into my Western Hockey League career and I was pretty sure it would now be over.

I was frustrated with my poor decision. I dejectedly headed off the ice to take what I assumed would be my place on the bench for the rest of the night, waiting for a verbal assault reminding me again of my stupidity. I stepped into the players' box and sat down with my head drooped and my stomach churning, waiting and bracing for the inevitable. Then, in one brief and crucial moment, everything changed.

To everyone around me and even the coach himself, this moment was insignificant. He looked over at me sitting there with my long face and asked, "What are you doing?" As an expression of self-indictment, I answered,

"Didn't you see what I just did?"

His response was, "Yeah, don't do it again; get back out there." I was stunned. His answer changed my life.

Not for several years had anyone in the game verbally extended encouragement and confidence in me. That one simple sentence spoken by the right person at the right time radically altered my perception of myself as a player and more importantly, as a person. I have since said many times about that night forty years ago, it not only changed my life but *set the course* for my life. The words "Get back out there," established the belief in my mind that I could do this.

The remainder of the season turned out to be a very successful one for me. I received the Top Defensemen award at the end of the year and was appointed an alternate captain on the team because of the confidence and leadership I demonstrated. Few other experiences in my life have had the level of impact that night did. Countless times over the years I have reflected on that moment and reminded myself, "I can do this, and nobody can tell me otherwise!"

What we say, how we say it, when we say it, and to whom we say it, matters.

This is What We Know
About the Power of Words

1) **Life and death are in the power of the tongue**

   From the fruit of their mouth a person's stomach is filled; with the harvest of their lips they are satisfied. The tongue has the power of life and death, and those who love it will eat its fruit (Proverbs 18:20-21).

2) **The words we speak bring healing**

   The words of the reckless pierce like swords, but the tongue of the wise brings healing (Proverbs 12:18).

3) **The tongue steers our lives**

   Anyone who is never at fault in what they say is perfect, able to keep their whole body in check. When we put bits into the mouths of horses to make them obey us, we can turn the whole animal. Or take ships as an example. Although they are so large and are driven by strong winds, they are steered by a very small rudder wherever the pilot wants to go. Likewise, the tongue is a small part of the body, but it makes great boasts. Consider what a great forest is set on fire by a small spark (James 3:2-5).

4) **Words create something out of nothing**

   And God <u>said</u>, "Let there be light," and there was light (Genesis 1:3).

5) **Words set the course for a person's life**

   Then Jacob called for his sons and said: "Gather around so I can tell you what will happen to you in the days to come" (Genesis 49:1).

The Source of our Spoken Words

A good man brings good things out of the good stored up in his heart, and an evil man bring evil things out of the evil stored up in his heart. For the mouth speaks what the heart is full of (Luke 6:45).

In Genesis 48, when Jacob called for Joseph's boys to come before him, he did two things; he laid his hands on them and spoke very specific words over them. The words he spoke were intended to either reveal the course of these boys' lives, confirm the course for their lives, or create the course for their lives. Regardless of the intent, it was the words themselves that Joseph was determined to receive from his dad. He was keenly aware that whatever his dad was about to say would impact his boys' journeys for the rest of their lives.

We know that Jacob's words were powerful and divinely valuable because Genesis 49 opens with Jacob calling for his other sons and saying, **"Gather around <u>so I can tell you</u> what will happen to you in the days to come."**

These men were not young, yet they fully engaged in the invitation, seemingly aware of the magnitude of what was about to be spoken over them.

What was Jacob drawing upon to have such profound influence in the lives of his family? Let's consider the sources from which Jacob drew this depth of wisdom and insight.

Jacob had:

1) Prophetic revelation

Jacob was clearly restating something he had heard the Lord put into his heart for those boys. Without sounding too mystical, there is no question that God places words, perspectives, and intuition into our minds that we could not have come up with ourselves. When you pray for your family and even when you are just thinking about them, ask God to reveal insights about the person that can help uncover the plans or encouragement Jesus has for them. Don't be afraid to share those thoughts and trust the Holy Spirit to confirm them in the hearts of your family members.

> The whisper of God's voice will never contradict His written Word

The whisper of God's voice will never contradict His written Word; hide His Word in your own heart and He will use the Scriptures as a guiding force in the revelations you receive. These prophetic insights will be the most influential and significant words you may ever speak over your family.

2) Experience—he had met God

I have a friend that said to me once, "I am now sixty-seven and I finally have something to say." There comes a time when we, through our very life experiences, finally have things that need to be said and need to be heard. Jacob had walked with God. There was no more theory or assumption, only real life. What he spoke came from the encounters he had with God. What he imparted was what he had personally witnessed and was now fully convinced to be truth.

Jacob had made grievous errors in judgment, had been blatantly disobedient, and yet had been faithful in his service and commitment to God. His mistakes had cost him dearly, and his loyalty paid him royally. The bottom line is he had pretty much seen it all. He knew first-hand the consequences of both choices.

As patriarchs, the treasures we have packed away in our memories, the things that have shaped us spiritually, emotionally, and psychologically are the foundation on which the next generation needs to build. Give them away.

3) Knowledge of his children

Train a child in the way he should go and when he is old he will not turn from it (Proverbs 22:6 NKJV).

It is said that this verse uses the imagery of a skilled archer selecting an arrow based on the bend of the material from which the arrow is crafted. Depending on the unique bend of that arrow, the archer would compensate his aim before releasing the projectile. Each arrow was different, therefore each time the marksman shot, the trajectory would be slightly different to hit his target.

Genesis 49 is an interesting study of how Jacob spoke a unique word of prophecy over each of his sons. He knew them intimately and addressed them, at least partially, according to their unique personalities.

Each of the children in your life is a masterpiece of God. The Bible says they have been *fearfully and wonderfully made*. Get to know them. Learn their unique bent. Submit their individuality to the Lord and hear what God might have for them specifically.

4) Convictions of best paths

For their command is a lamp and their instruction a light; their corrective discipline is the way to life (Proverbs *6:23* NLT).

Jacob's convictions were more than opinions. He knew truth. He knew the Word of God and had lived both sides of obedience. Scriptures clearly indicate that foolishness is in the heart of a child and that guidance, direction, and correction are a part of a guardian's responsibility to establish a healthy and wise pathway for the child.

Knowing the Scriptures and drawing on our own past choices, successes, and failures solidifies our understanding of how to speak strong words of encouragement and direction into the life of a young person.

5) Courage in his declaration

I love Jacob's strength when it came time to speak into the lives of his sons in Genesis 49. Basically, he ordered these grown men to *gather around because I'm going to tell you the way things are going to unfold in your life after I die.* There was no pandering to their feelings or carefully sidestepping the truth. He spoke about the things he saw in the spirit because his own days were numbered, and the success or failure of his family was at stake.

I am not suggesting for one minute that we not be gentle and full of grace when communicating with our children or grandchildren; on the contrary. What I am advocating is that we lead with boldness, understanding our position as the patriarch, and for the well-being of our family, speak with confidence and courage when declaring the things of God over their lives.

6) Recognition of his mantle of anointing and responsibility

I have spoken at length throughout the book about the role we play as patriarchs in our families. I don't need to restate this reality. I do, however, want to express with great fervor the truth that God has placed an anointing on the patriarchs to fulfill His purposes and plans for each generation. That anointing is divine and it is released when we operate effectively in our role. We may not always FEEL anointed, but in the unseen realm, that authority is recognized and honored. The Kingdom of God accompanies His own order and bestows favor and blessing when we function according to His ways. Embrace your placement and respect the mantle that rests upon you. You don't have to be the smartest guy in the room, but you do need to appreciate the mandate placed upon you.

What Do We Speak Over Our Children?

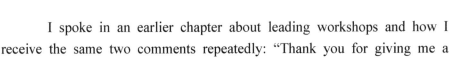

I spoke in an earlier chapter about leading workshops and how I receive the same two comments repeatedly: "Thank you for giving me a place," and "I don't know what to do." Too often, as men, we find knowing what to say or even how to pray over our grandchildren difficult.

Give some thought to this experience and ask the Holy Spirit to lead and guide you. James stated emphatically,

> God will unfold deep insights and realities that will penetrate the heart

"If any of you lacks wisdom, you should ask God, who gives generously to all without finding fault, and it will be given to you" (James 1:5).

If you prepare yourself prior to speaking over the lives of your family, God will unfold deep insights and realities that will penetrate the heart of the child for the rest of their lives. This is no small task. Proceeding without God's leadership limits the impact you can have on them.

The following guidelines will help serve as a roadmap to effectively deposit influential impressions and principles into the core being of your family members. What a profound responsibility and privilege to be used by Jesus this way!

1) Be Specific

When Jacob spoke over each of his sons in Genesis 49, he did not use generalities in what he said. He clearly addressed the individual based on what he saw and what he understood to be relevant for that specific man.

When we speak in vague and general terms, the child will disengage and consider the prayer to be irrelevant. By focusing on the distinctive and exceptional aspects of the child's own journey, we capture an opportunity for inspiration like few other moments in time. It's those moments and those words that become cemented into the developmental influences of who they will become as they grow up.

Being specific requires that we build a relationship and be aware of the challenges and potential of each child. Ask questions and pay attention to the environment. By being attentive you will gain insight that can prove to be significant in your communicating God's blessing over them.

2) Use Trent / Smalley Temperament Analysis

John Trent and Gary Smalley have done a marvelous job of using animals as a means of defining the character traits of children.

▶The Beaver typifies the analytical, self-disciplined, yet moody and often negative person.

▶The Lion is the strong-willed, decisive yet domineering and unemotional type.

▶Then there is the Otter. This person is outgoing and talkative but can be undisciplined and given to exaggeration.

▶Finally, the Golden Retriever; easy going and calm but also indecisive and often given to procrastination.

You can learn much more about this temperament study in the book *The Two Sides of Love*, by Smalley and Trent.[14]

When speaking over our children, these caricatures can be useful in affirming their strengths while riveting the unique design of God into their minds. The fact that each person is special and fearfully and wonderfully made, is an important reality and truth for every individual to embrace and appreciate about themselves.

3) Be Prophetic

The concept of the prophetic word is often viewed differently by different people, holding slightly different perspectives of the way the Holy Spirit interacts with us. Some believe it should be solely a reiteration of the written words of Scripture, and others believe there is room for promptings or impressions in your thoughts, inspired by the Holy Spirit, that are specific to a person or situation. Regardless of your convictions, one thing is certain. The

---

[14] Smalley, G and Trent, J, PH.D. (1990). *The Two Sides of Love*. Carol Stream, Illinois: Tyndale.

prophetic word will never contradict the written Word and must always be confirmed by the Scriptures.

One of my favorite verses in the Bible is the record of Jesus' encounter with Peter when He first met him and identified the potential in him in John 1:42. **"He brought him (Peter) to Jesus. Jesus looked at him and said, "You are Simon the son of John. You will be called Cephas" (which when translated, is Peter).** We know what Jesus spoke was a prophetic revelation, but it was also a declaration. The name *Simon* in the New Testament was a baby name and implied immaturity and in some ways, weakness. *Cephas* meant *Peter* or *Petros* which means "a rock." He was saying, Peter, you are going to be an important player in my plans.

I heard an old preacher once describe this conversation as Jesus declaring over Peter, "You are currently a pebble, but you are going to be a big, strong rock." I like that. Jesus was creating in Peter's thoughts and spirit, the imagery of what God had planned for him.

I strongly recommend that you speak positive, life-shaping prophetic words, or words you believe are consistent with the Scriptures, over your children. Literally, pray Bible verses over them.

4) **Speak Vision**

What do you see when you look at your grandchildren? Be careful about limiting them or your own perspective of what God might want to do with them. Dream big. Speak big and cast a large vision for your family.

I am always intrigued by the way certain families tend to follow the patterns of the previous generation. How is it the Bush family can have both a father and a son become president of the

United States? Is it because they were smarter than anyone else? I won't attempt to answer that. The only explanation, is vision. George W. saw what his father did, and I am sure he was encouraged and convinced by his father and others that it was entirely possible, and even probable, that he could be president as well, if he wanted. You don't achieve that position without someone instilling in you the original vision.

We can establish a pathway to greatness for our families through the spoken words of profound, life-altering vision. Don't be timid. A life can achieve that which a mind can conceive. A mind can conceive world-changing vision when an appropriate word of encouragement is planted.

5) Speak life

Be positive and encouraging. Guard against anything that can tear down. If life and death are in the power of the tongue, choose life. Love, joy, peace, patience, kindness, goodness, gentleness, faithfulness, and self-control are the fruit of the spirit. Everyone wants these for themselves and for their family. Words that reflect these characteristics will help reaffirm the work of God in any person's life. It is a wonderful privilege to participate with the Holy Spirit in seeing that fruit blossom as part of your child's personality and worldview.

6) The "Prayer of Blessing"

When I hear men say, "Help me to know what to do," I direct them to the "Prayer of Blessing." This prayer is a compilation of the many places in Scripture where someone spoke blessing into the lives of individuals or even over the nation of Israel. I have

The sidebar note reads: We can establish a pathway to greatness for our families

summarized these blessings into five categories, as previously noted. Here, we will revisit them from a more personal perspective.

a) The **KNOWLEDGE** of God

The Apostle Paul prayed that the church of Ephesus would have an experience with God not unlike his own. He specifically prayed that the **eyes of their understanding would be opened** and that they would **know God**.

When a person has their own personal encounter with Jesus, their lives will never be the same. Sunday school stories, healthy home representation of Christ, and strong influencers are all essential elements of raising someone to walk with God, but when that person's life is transformed because of an intimate revelation of the grace of God and the love of Jesus, they will certainly walk faithfully with Him.

Pray over your children that they would KNOW God (Ephesians 1:17-18).

b) The **POWER** of God

Jesus commissioned the disciples to wait in the city until they were **"clothed with power"** (Luke 24:49). The book of Acts is a historic collection of how God filled His people with His Spirit, empowering them to proclaim the gospel and to change the world. Jesus declared that for those who are thirsty and who believe in Him, **rivers of living water shall flow from within you, and this He spoke of the Spirit** (John 7:38-39).

As the patriarch in your children's journey with Christ, it is an awesome privilege to pray with them to receive the anointing and infilling of the Holy Spirit, to see that river of living water flow out from them as they experience God's <u>POWER</u> for themselves.

c) The **FAVOR** of God

John prayed for his friend Gaius, that he would be **in good health and that he would prosper as his soul prospered** (3 John 1:2). The subject of the favor of God is a consistent theme throughout the Scriptures. The longing of every person's heart is that they would live under the covering, protection, and care of God and that His favor would be obvious in all they and their family do.

I suggest you pray for your family that God would add His favor to their:

- Health
- Finances
- Relationships
- Protective care from anything that may cause them harm

d) The **PURPOSE** of God

What is God's plan for your children's lives? How does God intend to use them for His Kingdom? There can be no greater fulfillment than to understand the call of God on our lives and to serve Him faithfully and obediently in that call. Every human being has unique gifts, abilities, and desires, that when coupled with the power of God, unveil the destiny and purpose Jesus urges them to fulfill. Knowing what that purpose is comes through promptings of the Spirit. Whether large or small, the understanding of God's call matters.

Grampa, play your part by praying that the PURPOSE of God may be discovered by your children.

Pray their hearts will not rest until they engage completely in that call.

e) The **DESIGN** of God

In a society that so desperately wants to mess with the identity and individuality of young people, it is more important than ever that we encourage our children to embrace **God's** unique design of who they are. The Psalmist wrote that they are *"Fearfully and wonderfully made"* and God told Jeremiah that He had **formed him in his mother's womb (Jeremiah 1:5).**

Our children and grandchildren need to know how special and unique they are according to God's design. We need to pray that there be no confusion as to who or what God has created them to be. Jesus challenged people to **love their neighbors as they love themselves** (Mark 12:31). Having a healthy, accurate appreciation and love for themselves enables them to have a joyous and godly perspective on the world in which they live.

They are the unique, specific, and exceptional DESIGN of God. May they see it and embrace it as their gift from the Lord.

Grampa, do you have something to say?
Say it like your children's lives depend on it … because they do.

BELIEVE GOD for the TRANSFORMATION

Chapter 11   STEP #5

Without Faith It's Impossible

"And without faith it is impossible to please God, because anyone who comes to him must believe that he exists and that he rewards those who earnestly seek Him."

Hebrews 11:6

IN 1986, MY WIFE MARY AND I HAD THE PRIVILEGE OF JOINING A SMALL group of people who had gone into a community to plant a new church. They were a vibrant group of young families with tremendous energy and vision to establish a lighthouse in their new surroundings where they could raise their families and live out their faith. They had chosen an upstairs office space to gather every Sunday morning to worship and to serve as their church home for weekly activities. I remember the first time I went there and climbed the long, narrow, dark stairwell leading up to the small meeting room. It was cozy, with a very low ceiling and large windows facing out onto the street. I remember those windows being a great indicator of whether I was preaching well or not, because if I wasn't, the people would be staring out of the window, distracted by whatever was happening across the street in the parking lot. Like I said, it was cozy, maybe too cozy for a young pastor's liking. Even though the atmosphere was quaint and serviceable, it soon became obvious the space was not adequate for the growth of the church nor the expansion of our growing families; it was time to move up.

Within a couple of years, these young, progressive and visionary leaders began to pray and believe God for a facility that would accommodate the continual multiplication of our assembly. Through a lot of creative thinking and sacrifice, we eventually secured land that would inevitably become the church building we could call our own. The challenge was significant and the cost of construction clearly beyond our immediate means. The only way that property could become a reality for us was to gain the confidence of a lending institution that would provide us with the necessary finances to proceed with our plans. Fortunately, there were some successful businessmen in the group that had both the expertise and connections to guide us through the process of securing the necessary resources required to proceed with our vision. We met with the banker, negotiated the terms, and convinced the lender that we were, in fact, a good investment, and that we would indeed be capable of meeting our end of the contract.

It was an exciting time. The agreement with the bank to fund our building project was the basis from which all future dealings could go forward. The architect, the excavation, the building materials, and all other contracts could be approached with certainty because we had assurance from an unequivocal source of provision, affirming we could meet our obligations. It had nothing to do with our personal word or enthusiasm, but rather, everything to do with the documents from the bank stating they would cover us in the venture. The vision of our own church building where we could grow our congregation and impact our community could all become a reality because of that contract with the bank. It was our "title-deed." Not a single individual in the group could pay for one part of the project on their own. With the backing of that institution, however, which was more than able, we marched on undaunted with the construction of our brand-new facility. And even though there was nothing yet standing, "by faith," we could visualize every aspect of our yet to be realized worship center. The excitement was palpable because we knew it was just a matter of time before our dream would be an actual, physical reality. We had confidence based on a promise from a source bigger than ourselves.

> Now <u>faith</u> is the <u>assurance</u> of things hoped for, the <u>conviction</u> of things not seen. For by it the people of old received their commendation.
>
> Hebrews. 11:1-2 (ESV)

This verse has always captivated my interest. What does it mean and how is it relevant to us in our role as dads and grandfathers?

This is how A.T. Robertson, the renown Greek scholar, defines faith in Hebrews 11:1.

Hupostasis is a very common word from Aristotle on and comes from upisthmi (upo, under, isthmi, intransitive), what stands under anything (a building, a contract, a promise). See the philosophical use of it in 1 Thessalonians 1:3, the sense of assurance (une *assurance certaine, Mngoz), that steadiness of mind which holds one firm (2 Corinthians 9:4). It is common in the papyri in business documents as **the basis or guarantee of transactions**. "And as this is the essential meaning in Hebrews 11:1 we venture to suggest the translation 'Faith is the title-deed of things hoped for'."[15]*

"Guarantee of transactions," or the "Title-deed of things hoped for." What marvelous imagery of what it means to have faith. Our "Title-deed" is God's Word. His promises give absolute assurance that He will fulfill the obligation. His Word is our hope. We can trust Him because He is faithful.

Twenty four times in Hebrews 11 the word *faith* is used to describe the great men and women of God who were holding a title-deed to a promise they had received from the Lord. Many, if not most, did not live to see the promise fulfilled. However, in God's time, those promises unfolded in the next or later generations.

> "being confident of this, that he who began a good work in you will carry it on to completion until the day of Christ Jesus."
> Philippians 1:6-10

Jacob was only days or even hours away from passing when Joseph brought his sons to him. Jacob knew he would not see the unfolding of his blessing in the lives of Ephraim and Manasseh. However, he understood the urgency of the impartation. As the patriarch, Jacob embraced his responsibility because he believed the promises would ultimately be fulfilled. Why? Because he knew God; he held a "title-deed."

The truth is, many of us will not live to see the full evidence of God's blessing in the lives of our grandchildren. What is true, however, is that we

---

[15] Robertson, A.T., (2000). *Word Pictures in the New Testament*. Nashville, TN: B&H Publishing Group.

have a "title-deed." When we speak blessing over our families, it must be done in faith: "<u>On the basis or guarantee of a transaction.</u>" When we faithfully honor the position, role, and responsibility of the patriarch in our grandchildren's lives, we enter into an agreement with God. When we pray, God hears and activates the process of doing His great work in them. That's our hope. That is our mandate. That's why we do it. It's because of the assurance of God's sovereign love and mercy. The fact that He loves our family members more than we do and longs to have them walk with Him is why this privilege of passing on blessing is so important.

As the family patriarch, you have a "title-deed" from Jesus relative to your children and grandchildren.

The Development of Faith

Faith is somewhat of a mystery for most believers. It can be hard to muster up the seemingly necessary emotion or enthusiasm to believe God for the results we want, especially during life's many challenges. When we read the "Hall of Fame of Faith" in Hebrews 11, we can't help but wonder, *how did they do it?*

Faith is a spiritual reality. It's the work that happens in the unseen rather than the seen. It's faith that precedes the victory on the field of spiritual combat. We march on toward that which we hope for, clothed in spiritual armor, holding high the shield of faith, knowing that the "Captain of Hosts" leads us forward. The assaults that are levied against us and our families can only be defended by faith. The progress and triumphs in life are secured by faith. We therefore need to understand the process of the development of our faith.

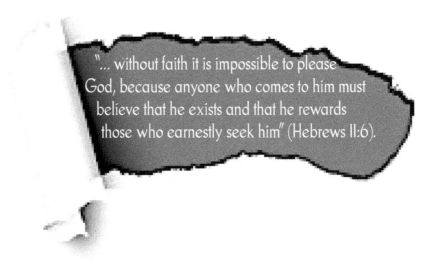

"... without faith it is impossible to please God, because anyone who comes to him must believe that he exists and that he rewards those who earnestly seek him" (Hebrews 11:6).

1) **Faith <u>COMES</u> by Hearing His Word**

> *"... faith comes by hearing, and hearing by the word of God"* (Romans 10:17 NKJV).

When my children were born, it was the most exciting experience I had ever had. I remember looking into the eyes of each one of my new babies and thinking to myself, *Wow they don't look anything like I thought they would.* I know I should've had something a little more profound for thoughts, but newborns, having been packed away for nine months, do not look anything like they will even in the few hours following their arrival. My point is, it's impossible to know what the future will look like for a child, or even imagine what their physical appearance will embody.

Every parent guesses and tries to figure out how tall they will be, what color hair, whose family traits will emerge, etc. The truth is, you cannot know until they grow up.

Faith is like an embryo. The Apostle Paul, the Apostle Peter, and the writer of Hebrews all exhorted the church to not remain spiritual babies but to grow up into adults by feeding on the Word of God. The basic DNA of the Spirit is birthed when we are born again, but we can't imagine the full extent of our journey when we are still spiritual infants. It is through His Word that we grow, develop wisdom, discernment, and a hearing ear for His voice. It is God's Word that creates the ability to trust Him and believe Him for elements of spiritual power of which nothing else is capable. His Word ignites life within our hearts because His Word is Spirit. It is the essence of who Jesus is. To be full of His Word is to be full of the Spirit of Christ.

Feed on His Word and let faith arise in your heart for the lives of your family.

2) **Faith is <u>BUILT</u> on His Promises**

Then Jesus declared, "I am the bread of life. Whoever comes to me will never go hungry, and whoever believes in me will never be thirsty" (John 6:35).

This is one of the most powerful statements in the entire Bible. These promises of Jesus are so often read almost rhetorically, with little attention given to the hope He is offering to all mankind.

Think about what Jesus said. *"Whoever comes..."* *"Whoever believes ..."* That means me. That means you. That means your grandchildren. *"Will never go hungry ... Will never be thirsty ..."* Never! Really? Jesus made the most eternally secure declaration of all time. He was giving all who would come and all who would believe, a God-breathed, Heaven-sent promise—His Word. It is His promises upon which our faith is built. Anchor your hope in the promises of God. The greater your understanding of His promises, the greater your ability to rest in the assurance of His blessing being extended to your family.

3) Faith is **DISCOVERED** Through Experience

Of the twenty-four times in Hebrews 11 the word *Faith* is used, twelve of those references make note of people's specific encounters with God as He moved them onward toward the promise of a better future.

Jesus is not interested in us simply sitting around dreaming of ethereal concepts or possibilities. It's through our stepping up and living out His directives we discover His faithfulness and divine activity in the joys and disappointments of real world stuff. The pleasure of believing God and watching Him uncover the impossible is what having a personal relationship with Christ is all about. *"... in Him, we live and move and have our being ... "* (Acts 17:28).

When we walk with Christ, He shows us His intricate participation in our lives. He opens doors and shuts windows along the path. When we travel together, we learn His ways and recognize His voice. It is how we gain the ability to trust.

Children bring highs and lows; that's just the way it is. The experiences we share enable us to witness the hand of God at work. Behind every encounter is the craftsmanship of a living, loving God. Even in the trying times, God is active. Trust and believe. Watch for signs and indicators of His involvement. When you see Jesus orchestrate the things only

He can, it will make trusting Him going forward that much more sensible.

4) Faith is <u>STRENGTHENED</u> Through Trials

Consider it pure joy, my brothers and sisters, whenever you face trials of many kinds, because you know that the testing of your faith produces perseverance (James 1:2-3).

There was a time when we, as a family, faced some significant crisis. The heartache and stress of that time seemed unbearable. I remember vividly the moment when I felt God lift the heaviness of the situation and insert a glimmer of hope into my heart. It was at that moment I understood His pursuit of our lives never stops. That ray of light from His Spirit gave us courage that nothing else could provide. In hindsight, the experience has proven to be one of the most valuable and important incidents in our entire pilgrimage as a family. It seemed insurmountable at the time, but when God breathes life into our soul, confidence and conviction rise on supernatural wings, enabling us to press forward into any battle. The pain of that occurrence forever altered our ability to believe Jesus in other major steps in our lives.

Get involved in your kids' lives, even when times are tough. It's in that arena where the faithfulness of a living God becomes real. It's in those times our faith demonstrates what it means to present our "Title-deed" and send the adversary packing. We are here to do business. Let's get it done.

5) Faith is <u>NURTURED</u> by the Testimony of Others

And let us consider how we may spur one another on toward love and good deeds, not giving up meeting together, as some are in the habit of doing, but encouraging one another—and all the more as you see the Day approaching (Hebrews 10:24-25*).*

One of the great joys of my life is when I receive testimonies from grandfathers and dads who have actively embraced the role of patriarch in their family. I often receive emails or even better, videos, showing a grandfather laying hands on his grandchildren and praying over them. To read or watch the satisfaction of these men faithfully fulfilling their mandate is immensely encouraging. Stories of the faithfulness of God being demonstrated in the life of someone they love elevates my faith and motivates me to believe the Lord for greater things in my own family and ministry.

God told Abraham that He would bless him but also make him a blessing. It is never acceptable in the economy of the Kingdom to merely be a receiver and not also a giver. Jesus wants to pour into our lives, but what we pass on is even more valuable. I was once told we are to be a pipeline, not a pool. People need to be encouraged in their walk with Christ because that is what nurtures our faith. Tell your story. Share with others the things you have seen Jesus do. Get together with other men and encourage them with your testimony. Grow in your faith and help other guys to grow in theirs.

Faith Lived Out

I've discovered over the years that most things we learn are a process and require step-by-step development before they really make sense and become operative. I believe faith is one of those realities. It is best understood when broken down into manageable components. What does it look like? How is it lived out in real life? When do I know that I am walking in faith? If we are going to effectively impart the blessing of God with authority, this process will inevitably lead us to a deeper awareness of the activity of the Spirit in our efforts.

Hebrews 11 is the textbook on faith. It is the framework of how faith works. If we are going to understand God's expectations regarding faith, we must follow the lives of the great sojourners recorded in this chapter. Each of them exemplifies what it means to follow God and His leadership throughout their personal history. Each was driven by confidence and expectation because of what they believed was the direction of the Lord.

1) **Faith and Vision**

     The characters in Hebrews 11 all had one thing in common—vision. They saw something that was not yet real. It was this divinely revealed vision that caused them to press on in their pilgrimage toward *a city whose builder and maker was God* (verse 10). Being able to see something in your heart even though it is not yet visible in the natural, is an integral part of faith. Not only should we anchor our faith to God's promises, but we should be asking for vision regarding each of our grandchildren.

My grandson is an analytical thinker. He processes things in detail before he feels comfortable moving forward with activities. He is a Beaver. Based on that trait, along with other elements of who he is, I have begun to formulate a vision for his future. I am believing God for certain things in his life because I see what can be and what will be.

People say, "We don't know what the future holds." That's only partly true. Of course, we don't know what pitfalls or opportunities the future has for them, but we do know what the Word of God says, and we do know that it is possible to speak into existence things that are consistent with His Word. Create a picture in your heart—a vision for your children's lives that is in harmony with what God wants, then hold fast to that vision forever.

2) Faith and Obedience

"The very weapons we use are not those of human warfare but powerful in God's warfare for the destruction of the enemy's strongholds. Our battle is to bring down every deceptive fantasy and every imposing defense that men erect against the true knowledge of God. We even fight to capture every thought until it acknowledges the authority of Christ" (2 Corinthians 10:4-5 J.B. Phillips N.T).

The metaphor the Apostle Paul is using here is that of a walled Roman fortress that in the natural, seems virtually impregnable. He is declaring that even though the fight seems impossible, it is still no match for the authority of Jesus. As in Ephesians 6, Paul emphatically proclaims that he does not wage war in the visible world but rather in the spiritual world. He boldly states he can and will destroy the devices that set themselves up against the promises and truths of God. He says in the preceding verses that in the natural he is a bit of a chicken but in the spirit, he is bold and courageous because he knows this isn't his fight. This is the power of God endorsing His own authority.

The theme of 2 Corinthians 10 is the violation of the purity of the gospel by people that were seeking to draw away believers from Paul's message of the gospel. They were creating doubt and deceit in this young church and in what Paul was teaching. He tells these leaders that their deception is a spiritual attack, and that he is going to fight every false thought and suggestion, making it submit to the authority of Christ. Many translations of Scripture use the word *obey* to define what Paul was saying. The word *obey* in this context comes from the concept of coming under the jurisdiction of a higher power—a lesser force subordinating itself to the pre-eminence of another.

Faith is just that. Regardless of circumstances or situations, we are to bring opposing thoughts and emotions into the submission of Christ. We are to subject them to the highest power. Nothing overrules His Word.

We may be unsure of ourselves as patriarchs at times, but our confidence is not in who we are as people. We are simply to surrender our thoughts and intents to the Word of God and His promises. Learn to fight in the Spirit by bringing *every opposing defense* to the Lord. Make every imagination that wars against God's desire for your children *obey*, submit and conform to truth.

3) **Faith and Action**

When I was a kid, there was an older gentleman who traveled around to churches doing "kids ministry." He was an eccentric character who did magic tricks, told captivating stories, and possessed all sorts of unusual gadgets and creatures. To be clear, this individual turned out to be anything but pure. However, it's still interesting the way God uses even the weakest vessels to influence our relationship and understanding of Himself.

One of the critters the old fellow owned was Pedro the turtle. Pedro was over a hundred years old; an incredible piece of God's innovations. What I remember about Pedro was that he spent most of his time recoiled inside his shell, safe and quiet. The only way to get him out and moving was to place a leaf of lettuce on the opposite corner of his bed in the aquarium in which he lived. When that lettuce was placed inside his dwelling, he would slowly push his head and legs out of his shell, so he could move forward toward his lunch. Once his head was fully extended he could advance, but not before.

Faith is a bit like a turtle. Unless we take action, we can't fully experience the leadership and activity of the Holy Spirit relative to our mission or plight. The pilgrims of Hebrews 11 continued to push forward and remained diligent in their pursuits because they believed God had the ability and desire to reveal Himself in those pursuits.

When we engage as patriarchs in the exercise of imparting blessing in our grandchildren's lives, we will witness God's participation in our actions. Too often I hear, "I do pray secretly for my kids," or "It's a personal or private role I play." That's not enough. Be overt. Get in the game. Push your head out of the shell and take action. Actively pursue every opportunity to lay hands on your children, to pray for them and be the "head" in their lives. Our action makes room for God's demonstration.

4) Faith and Patience

We do not want you to become lazy, but to imitate those who through faith and patience inherit what has been promised (Hebrews 6:12).

Waiting is a lost art in our culture. Many years ago, I had the privilege of touring some of the ancient Aztec ruins in southern Mexico. *Fascinating* couldn't begin to describe what is there: miles of fence, pyramids, places of idol worship, and cities constructed of river stone and rock all meticulously placed and secured with a combination of balance and mortar. It is awe-inspiring to look at. How in the world did they do it? The most bewildering part for me was the amount of work and the length of time it would have taken to complete such magnificent structures. One by one, those rocks would have had to be hauled from who knows where to the building site, then strategically placed within the schematic of the overall design; talk about patience!

Instant gratification is rare in the Kingdom of God. When Moses' mother placed him in the wicker basket, she didn't know what would become of her son, but in faith she had no choice but to patiently wait and watch as God worked His plan. It is not unusual in the Bible for there to be decades, if not centuries, between major recorded events. It requires great patience coupled with unshakeable confidence to see the intentions of God unfold in the lives of our grandchildren. When we speak God's blessing into their lives, we then must wait and trust the faithfulness of Christ to be displayed over time.

Most of us as grandfathers will not even be alive when the full work of the Lord is realized in our family members. That's ok. We play an integral part of this eternal journey for them. That's how God created it to work. Be patient. Let Jesus do His thing.

5) Faith and Thanksgiving

Thanksgiving is the key that unlocks and reveals the proof of our faith. When I have promised one of my grandchildren candy, they know I'm going to give them that treat. If they were to stand in front of me and continually ask for the candy even though I'm offering it to them, they would never receive it.

"Grampa can I have a candy?"

"Yes, take it."

"Grampa, can I have a candy?"

"Yes, here it is, take it."

"Grampa, can I have the candy?"

"Yes, for goodness sake take the candy from my hand!" The continual *ask* does not indicate confidence in my provision. When they say, "Thank you, Grampa, for the candy," and then reach out and take it, that's when I know they really believe the treat is theirs.

When I believe God's Word is true, and I have asked according to His will, I then begin to give thanks for the evidence of His promise.

As I look down the road of my grandchildren's lives, I have no idea what challenges they will face, but I know this! Scripture tells me that Jesus will do a good work in them and He won't quit until He is finished. Therefore, I don't have to continually ask Him to do a good work, but rather, I give Him thanks for the work He is doing.

"Thank you, Jesus, that You will introduce Yourself to my grandchildren. Thank You that You will fill them with Your Holy Spirit. God, I give You thanks for Your favor upon them and that You are revealing to them Your purpose for their life."

Faith is not faith until you believe enough to be thankful. When you give thanks, the answers are released in the unseen and will eventually be witnessed in the seen.

6) Faith and Hope

During the Second World War, at the age of sixty-five, Sir Winston Churchill became the Prime Minister of England. Even though he was a man of considerable intelligence and capable political ability, it was not those qualities that resulted in him being elected. The characteristic that endeared him to the English people was his almost supernatural ability to inspire hope.

Churchill's granddaughter, Celia Sandys, honored her grandfather in a speech given in 2012, saying, "The impact of my grandfather's words during World War II was more powerful than any weapon ... whether speaking in the House of Commons or on the radio, the effect was profound. So many people have told me how his speeches gave them hope when they were in despair."

Everyone knew the German forces were advancing across Europe at an alarming speed, and England was directly in their crosshairs. When it seemed all hope was lost and the people were gripped with fear, Prime Minister Churchill would take to the radio on an almost daily basis and speak to the nation, giving them assurance that they were going to ultimately be triumphant in spite of the seemingly overwhelming odds. His famous dissertation "... we shall fight on the beaches, we shall fight on the landing grounds, we shall fight in the fields and in the streets, we shall never surrender,"[16] became the rally cry of not only the nation of Great Britain, but the entire assembly of allied countries. It wasn't strategy that won the war; it was the inspiration of hope and courage that injected confidence into the hearts of ordinary people.

Much has been written about Winston Churchill, but author and poet [Alfred] Duff Cooper summed up the world's debt to this amazing leader in the following short poem.

'When ears were deaf and tongues were mute

You told of doom to come;

When others fingered on the flute

You thundered on the drum;

When armies marched and cities burned and all you said came true,

Those who have mocked your warnings turned almost too late to you;

When doubt gave way to firm belief and through five cruel years,

You gave us glory in our grief and laughter through our tears;

When final honors are bestowed and last accounts are done,

Then shall we know how much was owed by all the world to one.'

[16] Retrieved from https://winstonchurchill.org/resources/speeches/1940-the-finest-hour/we-shall-fight-on-the-beaches/

Hope deferred makes the heart sick ... (Proverbs 13:12).

When faced with the challenges of life, faith is what spurs us on with conviction that God is sovereign and able to do what we cannot. Without hope, we become crippled with stress, discouragement, and fear. Jesus said the devil comes to kill, steal and destroy but that He came to give us abundant life (John 10:10). It's those promises that inspire hope.

Faith makes all the other steps in the blueprint work. Without faith, everything else becomes empty words and frivolous activity. Faith is the gunpowder that launches the other elements into the unseen realm with authority and impact. It is faith that allows our hearts to rest and trust.

Section Three

THE COMMISSION

THE PATRIARCH'S CHALLENGE

Chapter 12

"You don't have to be great to start, but
you have to start to be great."

Zig Ziglar

IN THE GENESIS 48 ACCOUNT OF JOSEPH AND HIS FATHER JACOB, URGENCY
was the impetus of everything that took place. Joseph found out his dad was
dying and realized his boys needed to receive their grandfather's blessing
before he died. Jacob responded as urgently as his frail body would allow
when Joseph arrived, by getting up off of his death bed and laying hands upon
his grandsons, promptly transmitting his blessing into their lives. There was
no time to waste. The hour was late, and the resolve of both men was obvious.
It had to happen—now!

All great missions start with a common denominator—urgency.

When problems present themselves, it takes courageous men to
respond to the challenge and stand in the way of opposing forces. The battle
for our families and our faith is rapidly closing in around us. There is a war
being waged in the spiritual realm, targeting our homes and our role as
lighthouses to the world. We cannot lose hope or heart in this struggle. The
opportunity to stem the tide of darkness is presenting itself to each man and
patriarch that will accept the mission. God has a strategy that involves us as
the heads of our homes. To miss the call and forfeit the responsibility is to

place our children and grandchildren in jeopardy. Accept the mandate and engage in the fight. The Kingdom needs us now. The times are urgent.

One of the greatest men of valor recorded in the Scriptures is Nehemiah. Even though he worked for the king, Nehemiah was not a priest, he was not a nobleman, nor was he a politician or warrior. He was the king's cupbearer. He worked for the government; he was a civil servant. In other words, he was a relatively ordinary guy, much like ourselves or the men with whom we associate. Regardless of our placement in society, whether king or servant, we are all equal at the foot of the cross. As a coach once told me, "Everyone puts their pants on one leg at a time."

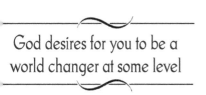

God desires for you to be a world changer at some level

God's choice of people to do His bidding is always curious to me. Nehemiah is a great example of how God, in His sovereign plan, placed this everyday kind of guy into the king's chamber to eventually fulfill His divine objectives through him. Nehemiah didn't realize what was happening. All he knew was there was something welling up in his emotions about the depletion of Jerusalem. It needed to be fixed and he was God's chosen guy. What happened next was obviously important enough to make it into the canon of Scripture. Never underestimate what the Lord is doing behind the scenes. You are in His plan. His purpose for you is to be a world changer at some level. Nehemiah turned out to be an amazing leader with divine favor and wisdom upon him.

A. NEHEMIAH IDENTIFIED THE PROBLEM

They said to me, "Those who survived the exile and are back in the province are in great trouble and disgrace. The wall of Jerusalem is broken down, and its gates have been burned with fire (Nehemiah 1:3).

The problem Nehemiah faced was that both the identity and the security of the nation were in peril. Nehemiah was moved in his spirit to do something about the situation, even though he was not someone with jurisdiction or even geographical relationship to the city of Jerusalem. He lived in the king's house.

As Christian men, we are being confronted with a similar spiritual battle. Our identity as believers is under intense assault. To be a Christian today in many parts of the world will cost you your life. In North America, the secular world has garnered a narrative of extreme bias and negativity against our faith and values. Walking with Jesus is becoming increasingly more divisive in a culture that has lost its way spiritually. Righteousness has become wrong and wrong has become right. As time marches on, the ungodly influences of our society continually gain momentum.

In 1975, Bill Bright of Campus Crusade and Loren Cunningham of Youth With a Mission developed a theory and strategy built upon what they called the, "Seven Mountains of Societal Influence."[17] It was their assertion that these seven areas were the foundation of any society, and that as believers, we have a mandate to influence these spheres with the message of Christ and His love for a fallen world. The seven areas of influence are as follows:

- Family
- Religion/Faith
- Education
- Politics/Law
- Media/News & Commentary
- Arts/Entertainment
- Business/Economics

---

[17] Bright, B. & Cunningham, L., *The Seven Mountains of Societal Influence,* Retrieved from https://www.generals.org/rpn/the-seven-mountains/

We don't have to do much analyzing to see that each of these areas has been significantly impacted by a profoundly ungodly and negative message. It appears Satan recognizes the potential in each area as well, and has been very intentional in his plan to commandeer control over them in an attempt to dethrone Jesus and destroy mankind.

Ignoring these realities is to place our children and grandchildren in harm's way. As men of God, it is our responsibility to recognize the situation for what it is and prepare to engage in this battle with vigor, strength, and conviction. The home is the foundation for all the others. As the patriarch, you have the ability to influence the role your children and grandchildren will play in each of the seven areas and the favor of God that will accompany them in their endeavors.

B. NEHEMIAH GRIEVED AND WAS COMPELLED TO ACT

When I heard these things, I sat down and wept. For some days I mourned and fasted and prayed before the God of heaven (Nehemiah 1:4).

When does the societal climate become severe enough to move men into action? How close to home will the darkness have to get before we say, "Not on my watch." Nehemiah was overcome with concern by the circumstances his community faced. He couldn't take it anymore. Something had to be done. You can literally feel the anguish in Nehemiah's writing. *I sat down and wept.* The injustice of the times consumed him and gripped him emotionally. It was like he couldn't think of anything else. *I mourned and fasted and prayed.* All this ordinary guy could think of was that his world needed God's help, and he was going to make himself available to correct the unacceptable conditions.

It's unfortunate that we get pacified by the "slow melt" of spiritual deceit because the consequences don't always have a direct impact on our personal world. The old adage "bad things happen when good men do nothing," applies today more than at any other time in our block of history.

God, help us to be grieved enough to compel us, as the *heads* of our homes, churches, and communities, to take action!

C. NEHEMIAH RALLIED THE ELDERS AND THE PEOPLE TO REBUILD THE WALLS

Then I said to them, "You see the trouble we are in: Jerusalem lies in ruins, and its gates have been burned with fire. Come, let us rebuild the wall of Jerusalem, and we will no longer be in disgrace." I also told them about the gracious hand of my God on me and what the king had said to me. They replied, "Let us start rebuilding." So, they began this good work (Nehemiah 2:17-18).

It was clear to Nehemiah that the undertaking was immense and that the cost was going to be high. The opposition was fierce, and the threats were real. There was no way this could be done without the participation of many capable, motivated, and gifted stakeholders. I love how this great leader appeals to the obvious in his call to the people most affected. *You see the trouble we are in.* He didn't isolate the situation just to his own observations. He included all who were impacted as one group. He didn't say "I'm the only one bothered by this." No, he emphatically beseeched his friends to look honestly at the situation and to engage in correcting the problem, regardless of how dire it appeared.

Men of God, we are being called to service. We are under attack and it is imperative we respond. The walls have been breached. The tactics of our spiritual enemy are diabolical, and the fight is at our door. The task is daunting, and the stakes are high but, *when we are weak, He is strong*, if we take our place and *resist the devil, he will flee from us.* The promises of our living Lord are so wonderful and encouraging. When we align ourselves with His ways we will be triumphant. A willingness to *see the trouble we are in* implores us to step up, link arms together, and push back the powers of darkness. *Let us start rebuilding.*

D. NEHEMIAH'S VISION AND INSPIRATION WERE BEYOND HIMSELF

After I looked things over I stood up and said to the nobles, the officials and the rest of the people, "**Don't be afraid of them. Remember the Lord**, who is great and awesome, and **fight for your families** ... " (Nehemiah 4:14).

All great leadership recognizes the responsibility they bear to move a group of people toward a better future. As Bill Hybels[18] refers to it, they are driven by a "holy discontent." They acknowledge things must change in current circumstances, and that they carry the mandate, opportunity, and anointing to lead the group into a new dimension or paradigm. Good leaders become captivated and inspired by a need for change, identify a solution, then fervently work toward mobilizing those they have charge over toward that hope.

As the patriarchs and men of God in our family structure, the mandate, opportunity, and anointing are incumbently ours to employ. Nehemiah gave an impassioned speech and plea to those that had joined him in this immense undertaking. The people were losing momentum, were weakened by fear, and had lost sight of the role God was playing in their mission. The enemy was taunting them, and it seemed as though the hurdles and barriers to success were beyond their capacity to overcome. The job looked overwhelming.

Where there is no vision, the people perish (Proverbs 29:18-27 KJV).

The most important role any leader plays is that of crafting and articulating compelling and motivating vision; helping people see what can be, what will be if they endure and press onward. They must passionately implore the questions, "What if, why not, and if not us then who?" Vision is seeing that better future, being convinced it can happen, and that things will

---

[18] Hybels, B., (2007). *Holy Discontent.* Grand Rapids, Michigan: Zondervan.

be different when we arrive. Nehemiah's courageous speech made the possibility of success seem plausible and worth the effort.

In the movie *Braveheart*,[19] William Wallace was zealously rallying his warriors to press on in the fight and to not tolerate or accept the tyranny of the English any longer. When provoked by one of his soldiers with the idea of surrender, he responded by saying, "You can surrender and live…. for a while, but neither you nor your children will ever be free." Our participation in this quest is not about us, it's about the next generations—your grandchildren and their children and their children's children. We are at the current pinnacle of our family trees. The choices we make today create a continual flow of favor on our descendants. Our engagement and dissemination of blessing in their lives now strengthens the cord that ties the spiritual lines of divine activity together for hundreds of years to come. What a powerful reality!

As we come to the close of this book, I am deeply moved and inspired by Nehemiah's challenge to his colleagues. It has become my own battle cry to men throughout our nations.

Nehemiah's 3 Point Challenge:

1. Don't be afraid

"Courage is not the absence of fear, but rather the judgment that something else is more important than fear." (Ambrose Redmoon[20])

Be courageous. Be the "Head." Be the leader in your family. Never surrender. Never give up.

Nehemiah acknowledged the reality of the opposition they were facing from their enemies and the impending threat they were

---

[19] Gibson, Mel, Alan Ladd, Bruce Davey, Randall Wallace, Sophie Marceau, Patrick McGoohan, Catherine McCormack, James Horner, and Steven Rosenblum. 2000. *Braveheart*. Hollywood: CA: Paramount.

[20] Keller, J., (March 29, 2002). *The Mysterious Ambrose Redmoon's Healing Words*, Chicago Tribune.

up against. He was smart enough to recognize the emotional pressure his people were under. Sometimes fear needs to be acknowledged for what it is, and threats need to be exposed for what they are in order for them to be overcome and be defeated.

Repeated throughout the Scripture, great leaders appealed to their followers with the call, "Don't be afraid. Be strong and courageous." Jesus buoyed the spirits of His own disciples with the promise, **"I have told you these things, so that in me you may have peace. In this world you will have trouble. But take heart! I have overcome the world"** (John 16:33). In John's instruction to the church regarding the false teachers that were trying to mislead new believers, he told them, *"**You, dear children, are from God and have overcome them, because <u>the one who is in you is greater than the one who is in the world</u>***" (1 John 4:4).

Sometimes we just need to be encouraged that we can do this; that future generations are depending on our courage and determination. I believe the Kingdom needs us now. Let's do it.

2. Remember the Lord

When I first began to serve Jesus and make Him Lord of my life, it was a revelation of the grace of God that transformed who I was and how I viewed my place in the world. An overpowering awareness of my sin and the absolute unconditional love and forgiveness of Christ was more than I could fathom. To this day, many decades later, the very thought of His grace makes me very emotional.

I can't begin to repay what Jesus has done for me. Nor does He want me to repay it. What He does want is for me to trust Him and follow Him. He wants me to believe He loves me enough to lead me through the landmines of both this world and the unseen realities amongst which we live. I need to trust that He can and will do for me the things that I cannot do for myself. He has taken complete control of my journey. He is Jehovah Jireh, **The Lord who has seen ahead and has made provision in advance.**

God asks for our obedience and willingness to be who He has called us to be—the rest is up to Him. As Nehemiah said to his partners, **"Remember the Lord who is great and awesome" (Nehemiah 9:32).** Our hope is in Him.

3. Fight for your families

In the movie *The Darkest Hour*,[21] Winston Churchill left his motorcade while en route to a meeting with the war cabinet, and intentionally used the subway train to travel to the parliament buildings. On the train, Churchill sat with the people who were living the best they could, despite the ominous threat of war. One by one he asked their names and looked them directly in the eye, wanting to see both what they were feeling and to transmit hope in return. When returning to government, he began the defense of his opposition to a peace agreement with Germany by reciting the names of the people he spoke with on the train. He took out a small piece of paper where the names of each of these individuals were written and clearly announced each name to the governing officials. He was putting a name to the blank faces of the people who would be affected by the decisions that were about to be made. Every person mattered. Every person was a son, a daughter, a brother, a sister, or a mom, or dad. The fight was so much more than a strategic battle of wits or supremacy; it was about loved ones.

Nehemiah stood before those who had joined him in the great task of rebuilding the city, in spite of what seemed impossible odds,

---

[21] McCarten, Anthony. *The Darkest Hour*. Film. Directed by Joe Wright. Universal City: Universal Pictures, 2017.

and put a name to every face represented by these workers. "**...
and fight for your brothers, your sons and your daughters,
your wives and your homes**" (Nehemiah 4:14).

Why does the *GRAMPA'S TIME* mission matter? It matters
because the very lives of Nixon, Callaghan, Kensington, and
Beckett depend on it. They depend on papa fulfilling his mandate
on their behalf. The future of these precious gifts from God lies in
the balance. I see their faces, I name their names, and I embrace
who they are as masterpieces created by a loving Heavenly Father.
Put the names of your own family on the list. Call their names out
loud. Take your place on the wall with like-minded brothers as we
rebuild that which the devil is trying to dismantle.

We will change the world.

Now is our time.

It's Grampa's Time.

> ## *The GRAMPA'S TIME Vision:*
>
> *To Enlist, Equip, Encourage, and Empower
> 1,000,000 grandfathers to lay hands on their
> grandchildren and to speak the blessing of
> God into their lives.*

The Prayer of Blessing:

In the Name of Jesus, _____, I pray the Blessing of God into your life.

1)   I pray that you would **KNOW GOD,** and that you would experience Jesus in a very personal and intimate way; that you would experience:

- Your own personal revelation of His amazing grace
- His forgiveness, mercy, and love
- The life-changing power of His Word
- The authority of the marvelous Name of Jesus.

2)   _____, I pray in the powerful Name of Jesus that you will experience and walk in the Almighty **POWER OF GOD:**

- That you will be full of the Holy Spirit
- That you will live under the Anointing of the Holy Spirit
- And that whatever you set your hand to do will see the authority of God released in you
- And that courageously you will know, live out, and proclaim the Righteousness of Christ in the world in which you live.

3)   I pray _____, that the **FAVOR OF GOD** will be continually on your life; that God's Favor will be on you and that you will prosper in every way:

- In your relationships
- In health
- In your finances
- And that you will live under the protection of the Holy Spirit from those that may seek to cause you harm.

4) _____, I declare that the **PURPOSE OF GOD** for your life will be fully revealed and fully employed in order that you may serve Jesus with boldness and clarity.

- I pray in the Name of Jesus that your heart will not rest until you walk in the fulness of God's call on your life.
- I pray that the advancement of the Kingdom of God will be your passion and that His anointing will enable you to serve Him all the days of your life.

5) _____, you have been "Fearfully and wonderfully made," you have been created unique and special in the wisdom and foresight of God. You are the specific and special **DESIGN OF GOD**.

- _____, God in His eternal plan has declared you to be the head and not the tail, to be a rock and not a pebble, to be blessed and to be a blessing.
- I pray in the Name of Jesus that you will, from this day forward, walk in the confidence of who God has made you and that your unique character traits and gifts will influence the world in which you live to turn to God and follow Him.
- May you understand your strengths and surrender them to the Lord that He might enable you to be all you can be.
- May you recognize your weaknesses and by the grace of God submit them to the Holy Spirit that He might help you to walk in self-control and obedience to Christ. You are special!!!

As I lay my hands on you now, may this Blessing be recorded in the heavens and be fulfilled by the grace and loving-kindness of Almighty God. Amen

MY PLEDGE

I, _____ , pledge to fulfill the role of Patriarch in my family and to faithfully impart this "Blessing" into my grandchildren's lives by laying my hands upon them and by declaring with my mouth that they might fully experience the Knowledge of God, the Power of God, the Favor of God, the Purpose of God, and the Design of God. By faith I believe that the eternal purposes of God will be fulfilled in them through this "Blessing."

NAME:_____

ADDRESS: _____

CITY:_____ POSTAL CODE:_____

EMAIL ADDRESS: _____

If you choose to join other men of faith to make this pledge a part of your personal life journey, please submit it back to GRAMPA'S TIME, in order for it to be added to the list of others who are committed to changing the world through their grandchildren. You can submit your signed pledge here:

Visit www.grampastime.com/the-pledge, fill out the form and submit online.

Important Note:

As we seek to fulfill the mission of influencing the lives of our grandchildren through the role of grandfathers and patriarchs throughout North America, I recognize that it will be impossible to do this alone. I am therefore, reaching out to each person that believes this is a significant and critical task and asking them to present the pledge to others that might share this passion and encourage them to join the pursuit of preparing the generations ahead for the glory of God. You can do this by simply directing these like-minded men to the website www.grampastime.com and having them commit to the pledge along with you. Thank you for your commitment to Christ and to the lives of YOUR grandchildren and children.

To receive your **FREE** *Grampa's Time* Self-study booklet, just email cal@grampastime.com and request a copy. I will gladly send you one if it will assist you in your journey of becoming the patriarch God has called you to be.

For speaking engagements, workshop presentations, or conferences, please contact Cal at calellerby@nucleus.com.

Watch for the upcoming small group study resource and other books designed to encourage and enhance your walk with Christ as the head of your home, your church, and your community.

The "Grampa's Time" ministry exists to:
"Enlist, Equip, Encourage, and Empower 1,000,000 Grandfathers and Fathers to Lay hands on their Grandchildren and Children, Speaking the Blessing of God into their Lives."

THANK YOU FOR THE
<u>SPONSORSHIP OF THIS BOOK</u>

Grampa's Time

"Enlisting, Equipping, Encouraging and
Empowering Grandfathers to Pray the
Blessing of God Into The Lives of Their
Grandchildren."

CPSIA information can be obtained
at www.ICGtesting.com
Printed in the USA
LVHW030511201218
601140LV00006B/6/P